Relaxation

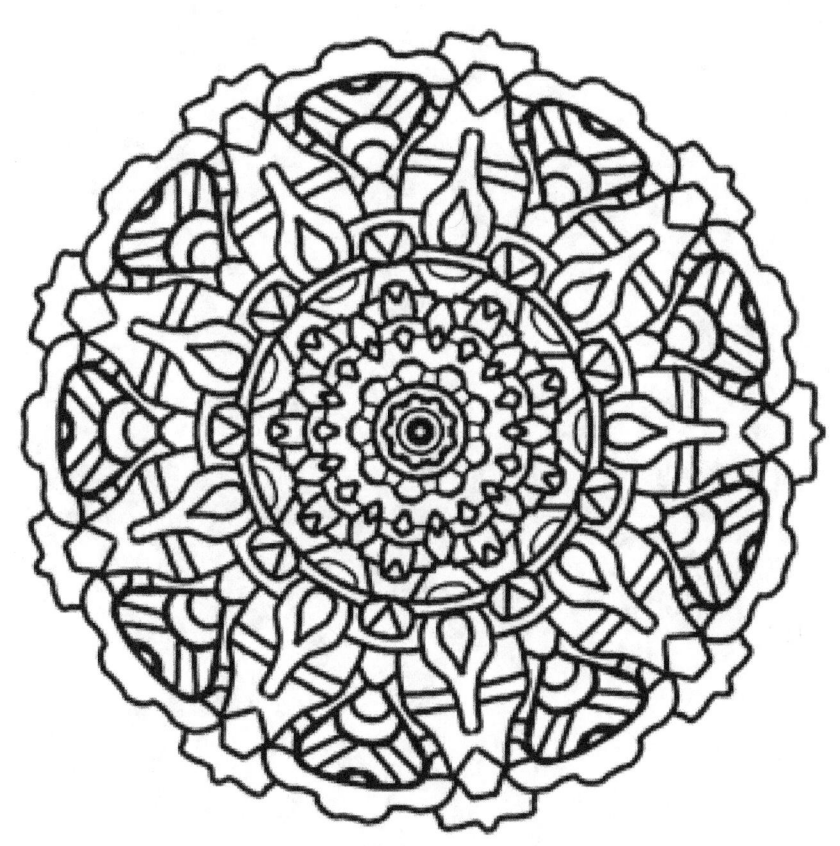

Adult Coloring Book Vol. 3

(c)2017 Serenity Reiki Clinic

Reiki Infused Mandalas to Help You Relax.

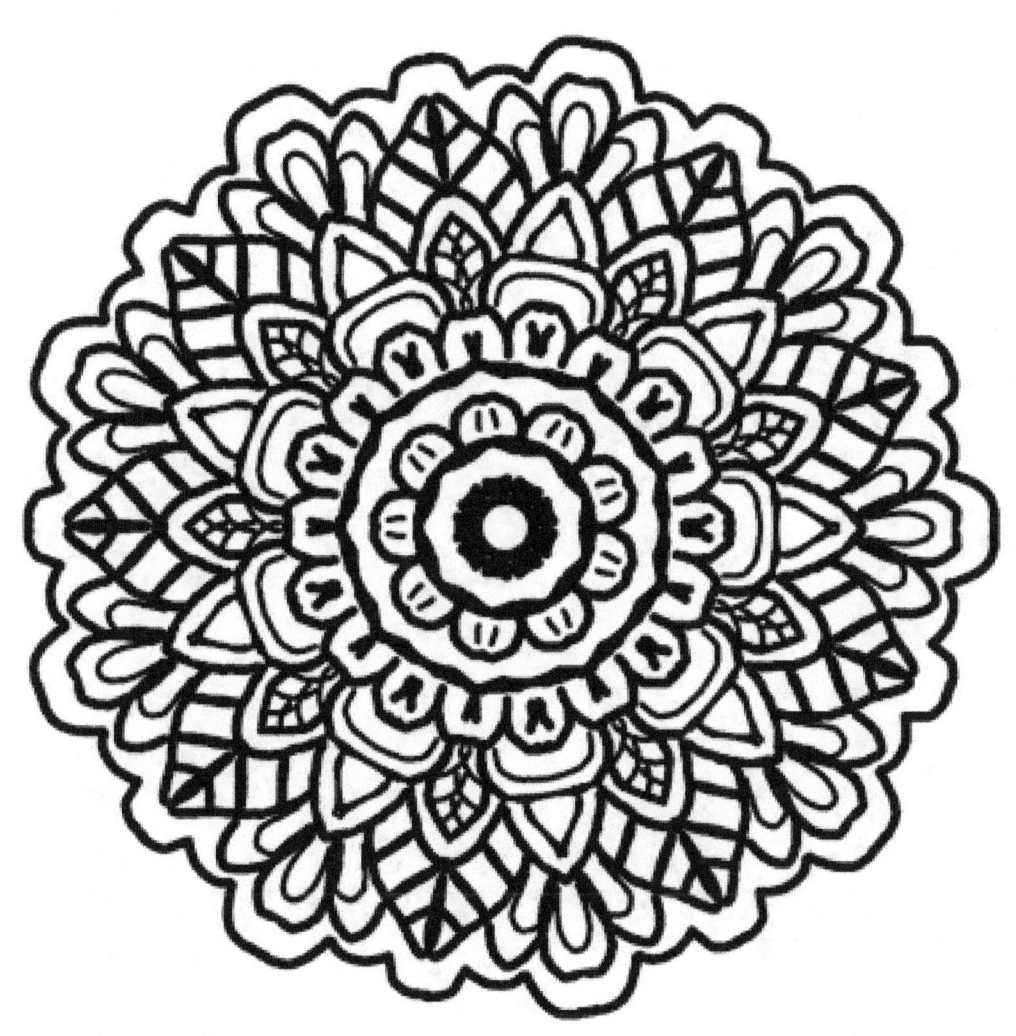

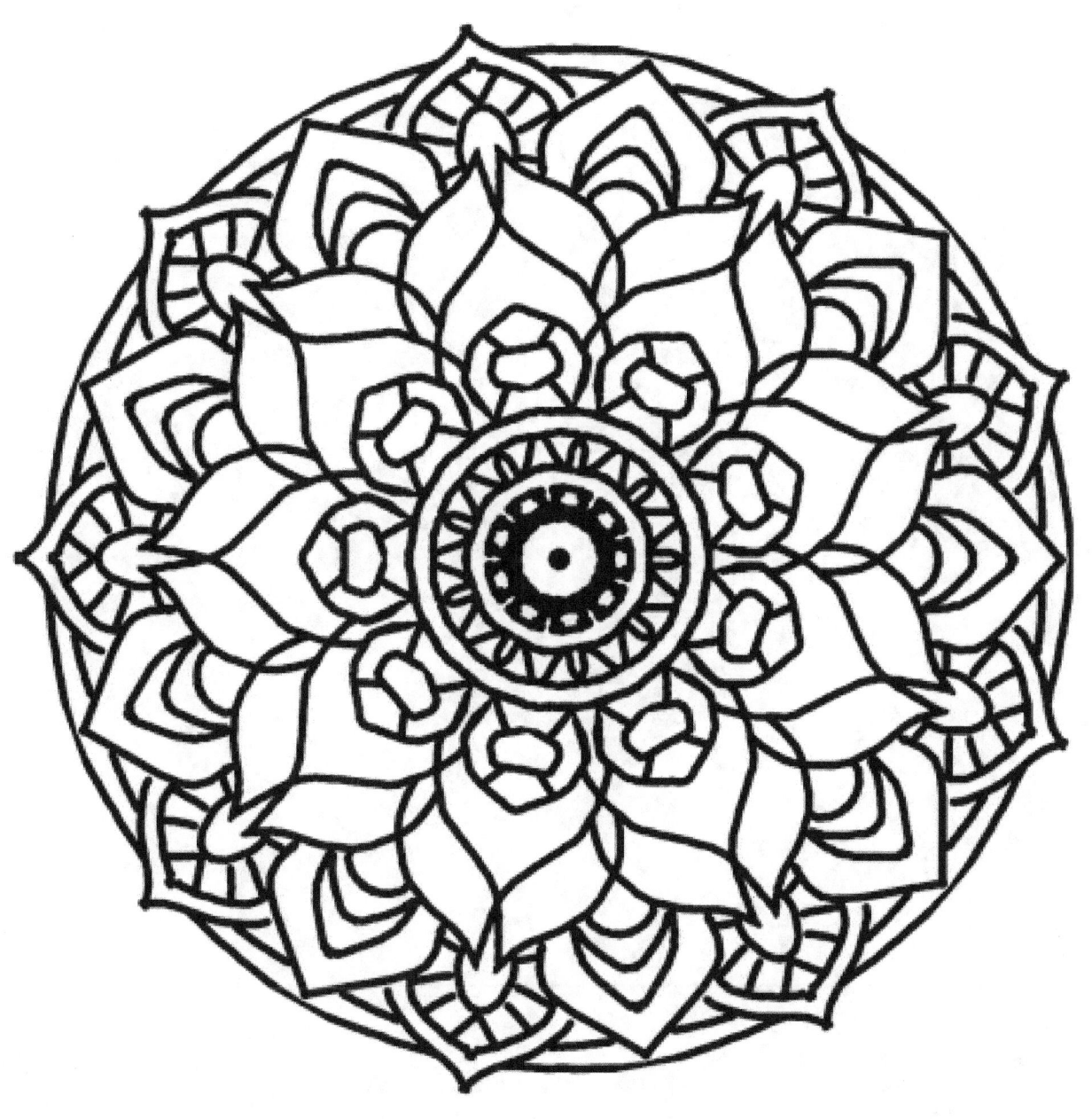

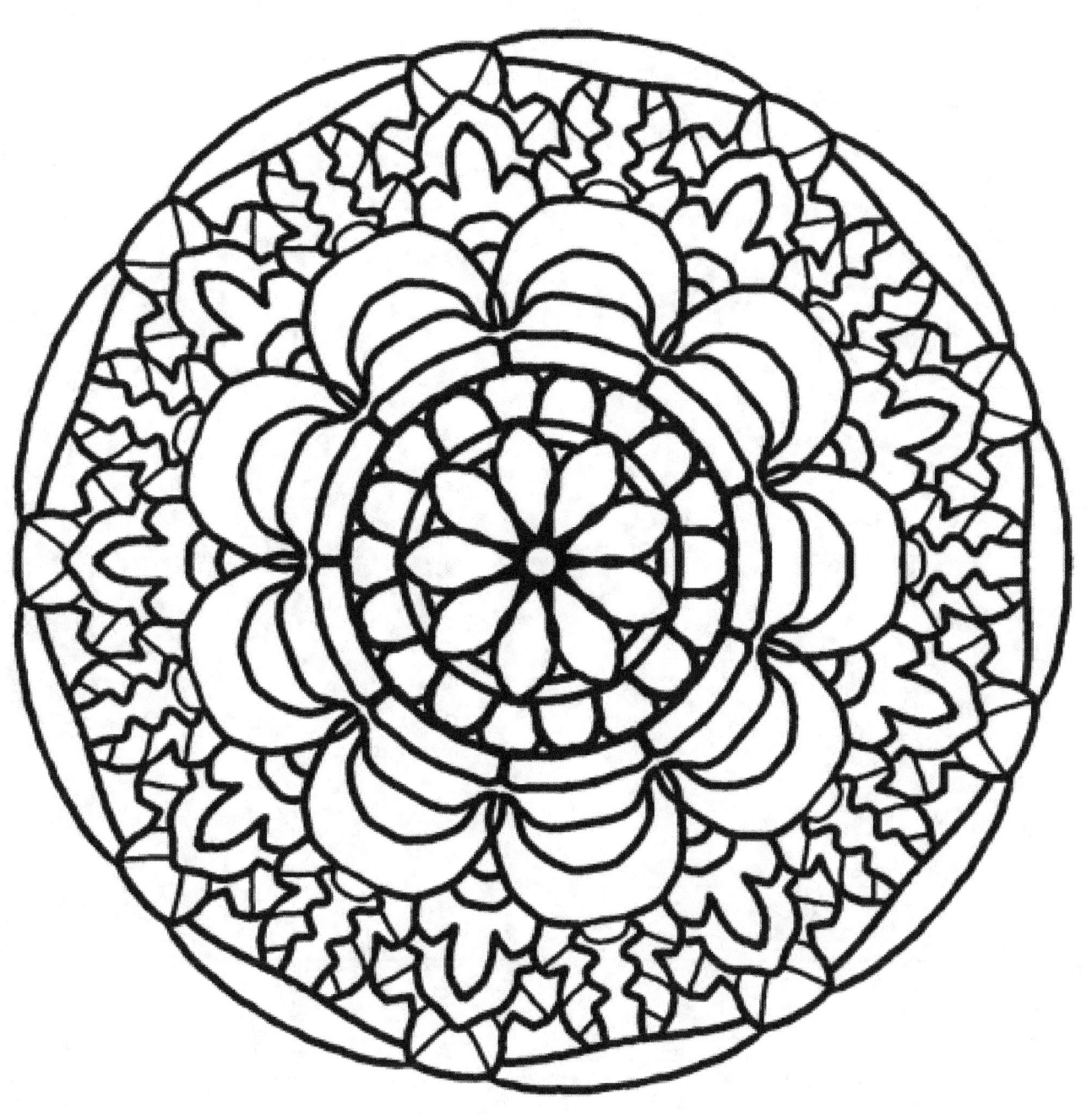

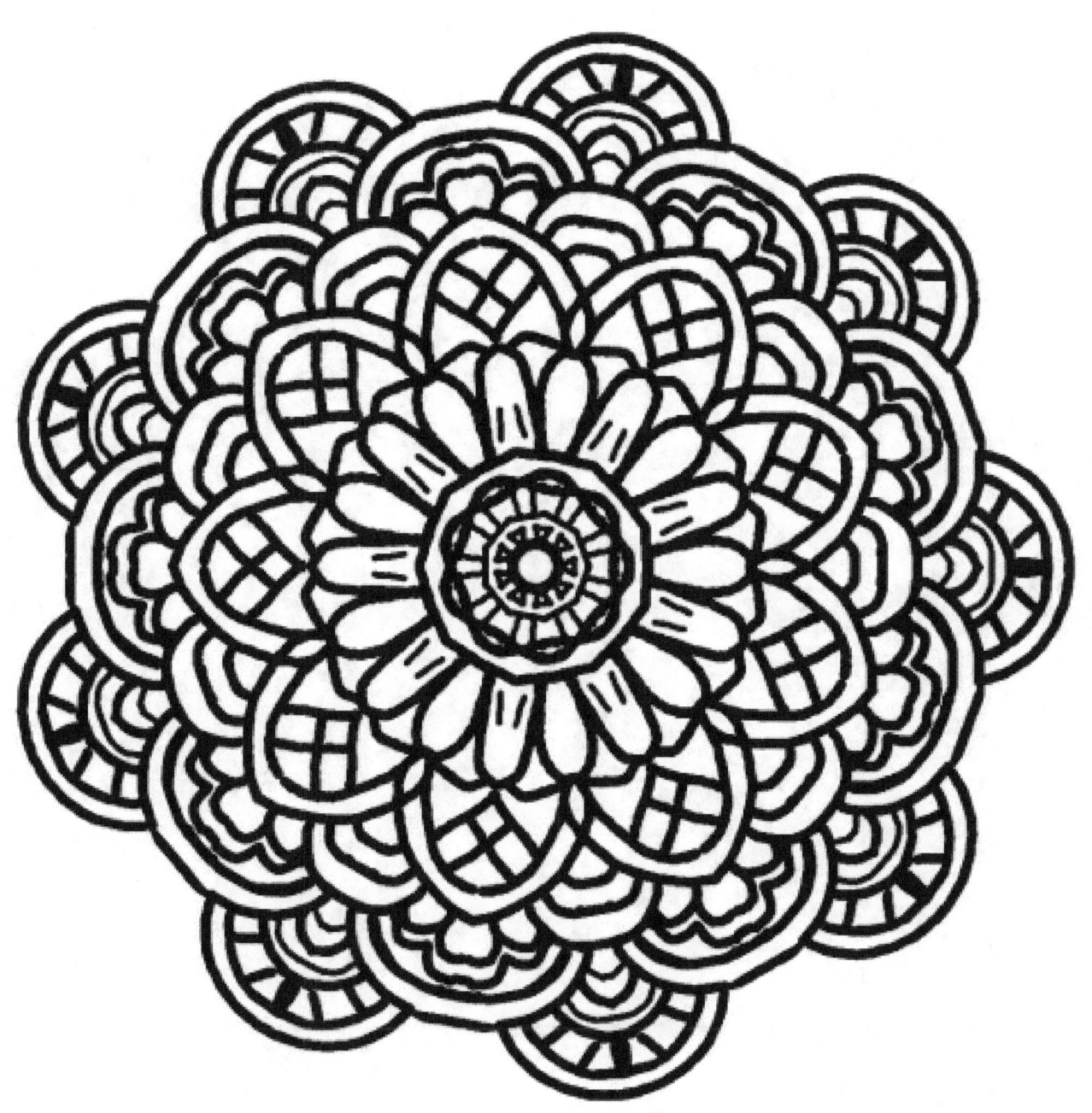

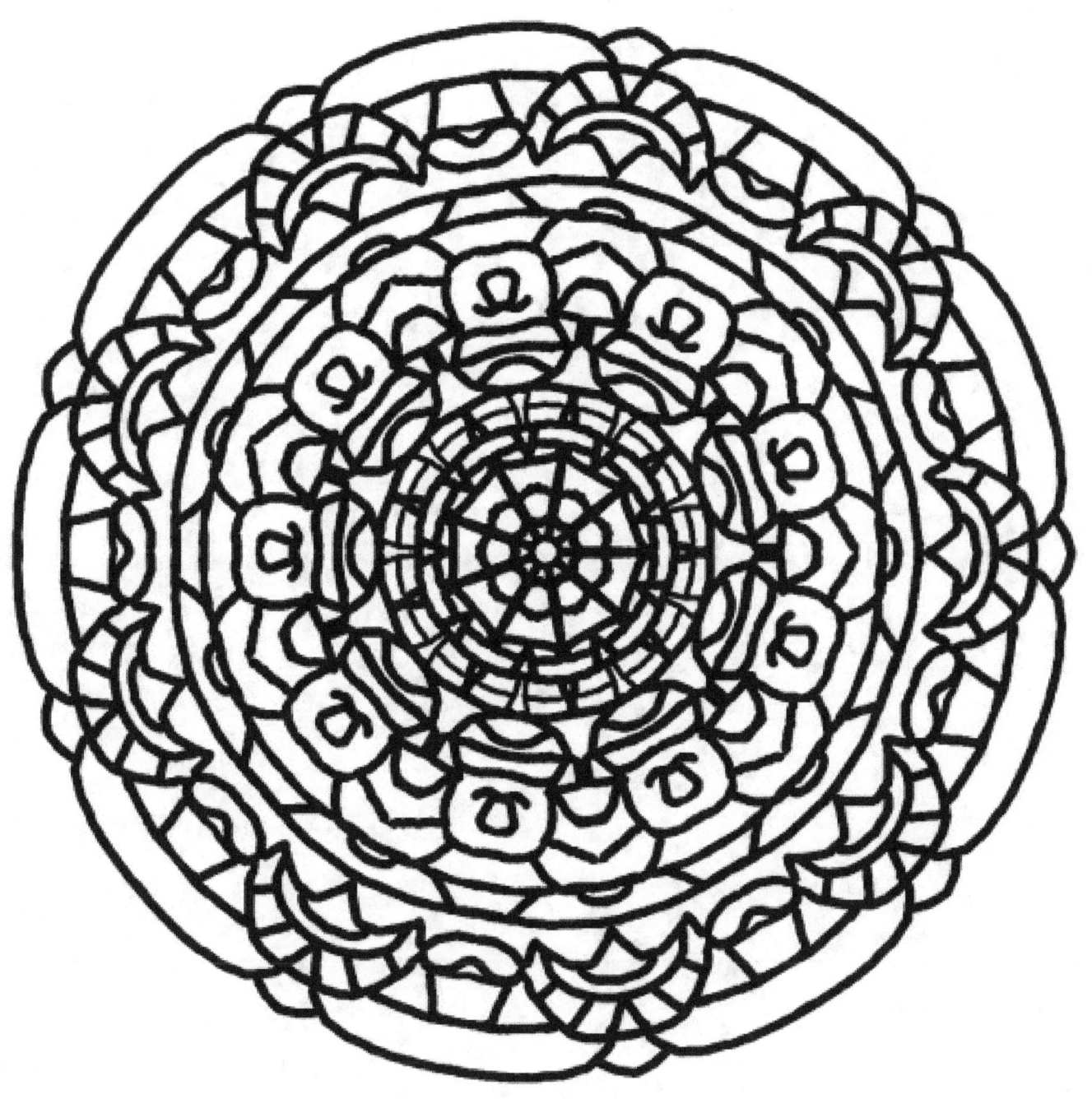

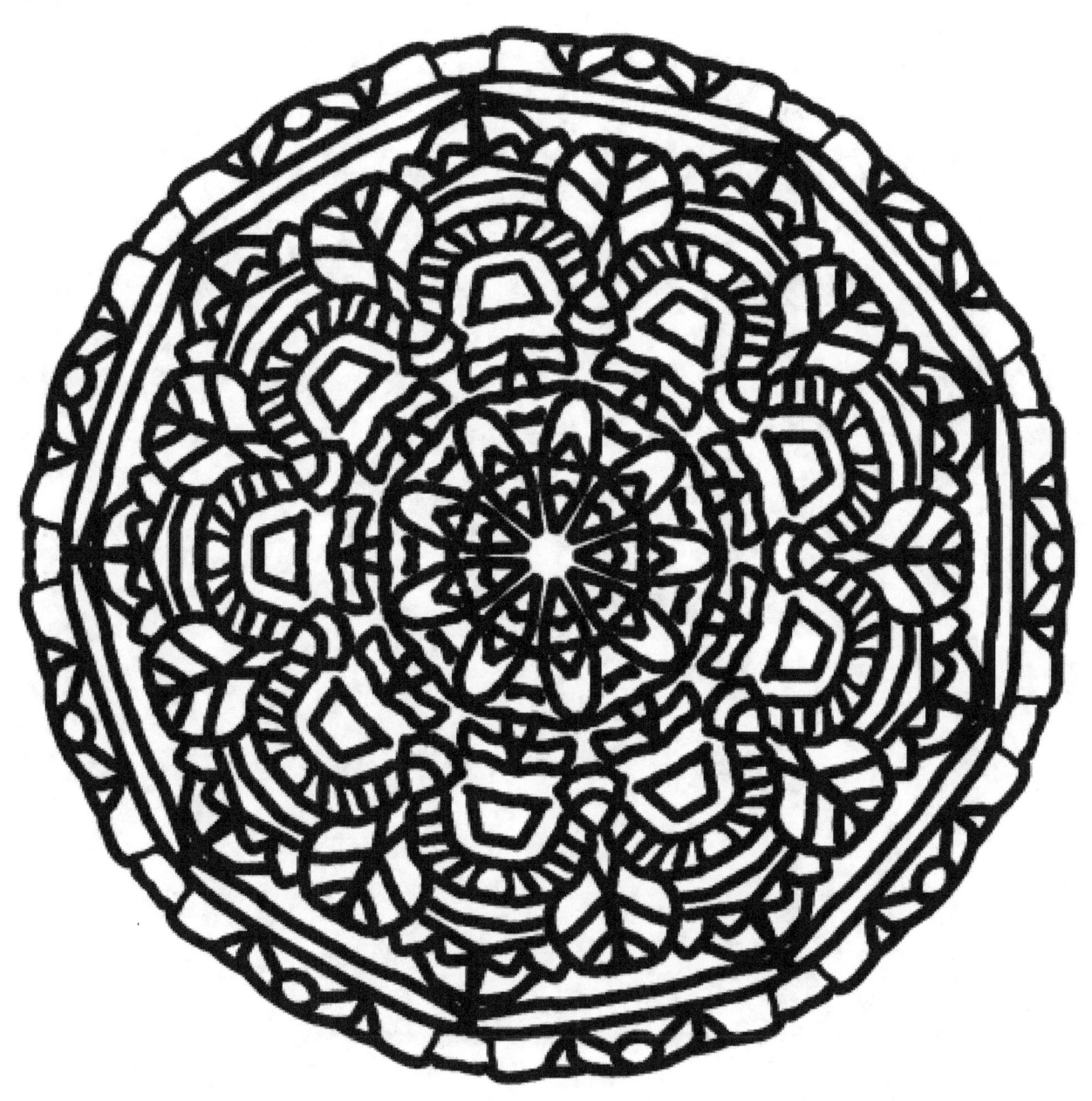

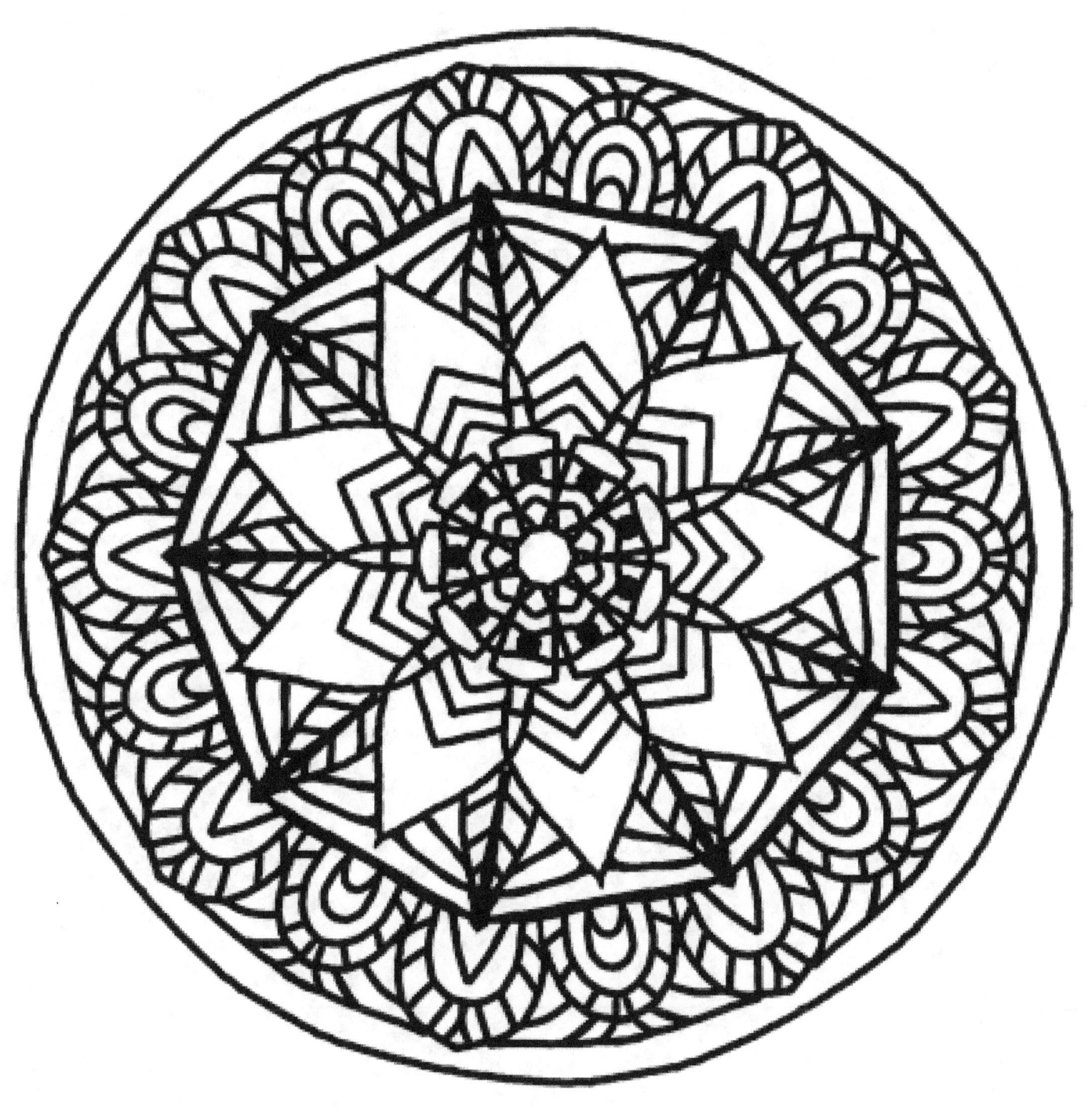

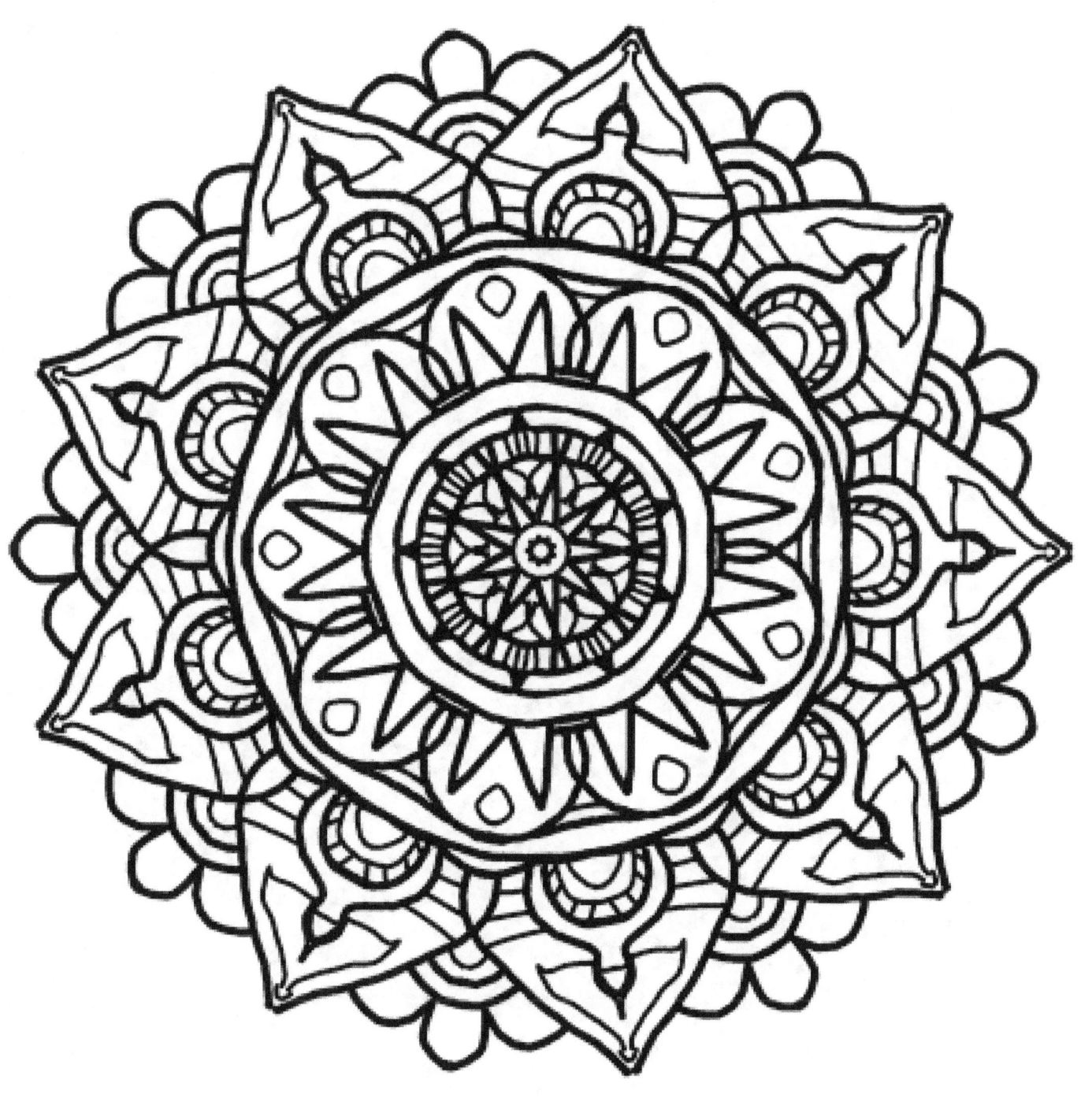

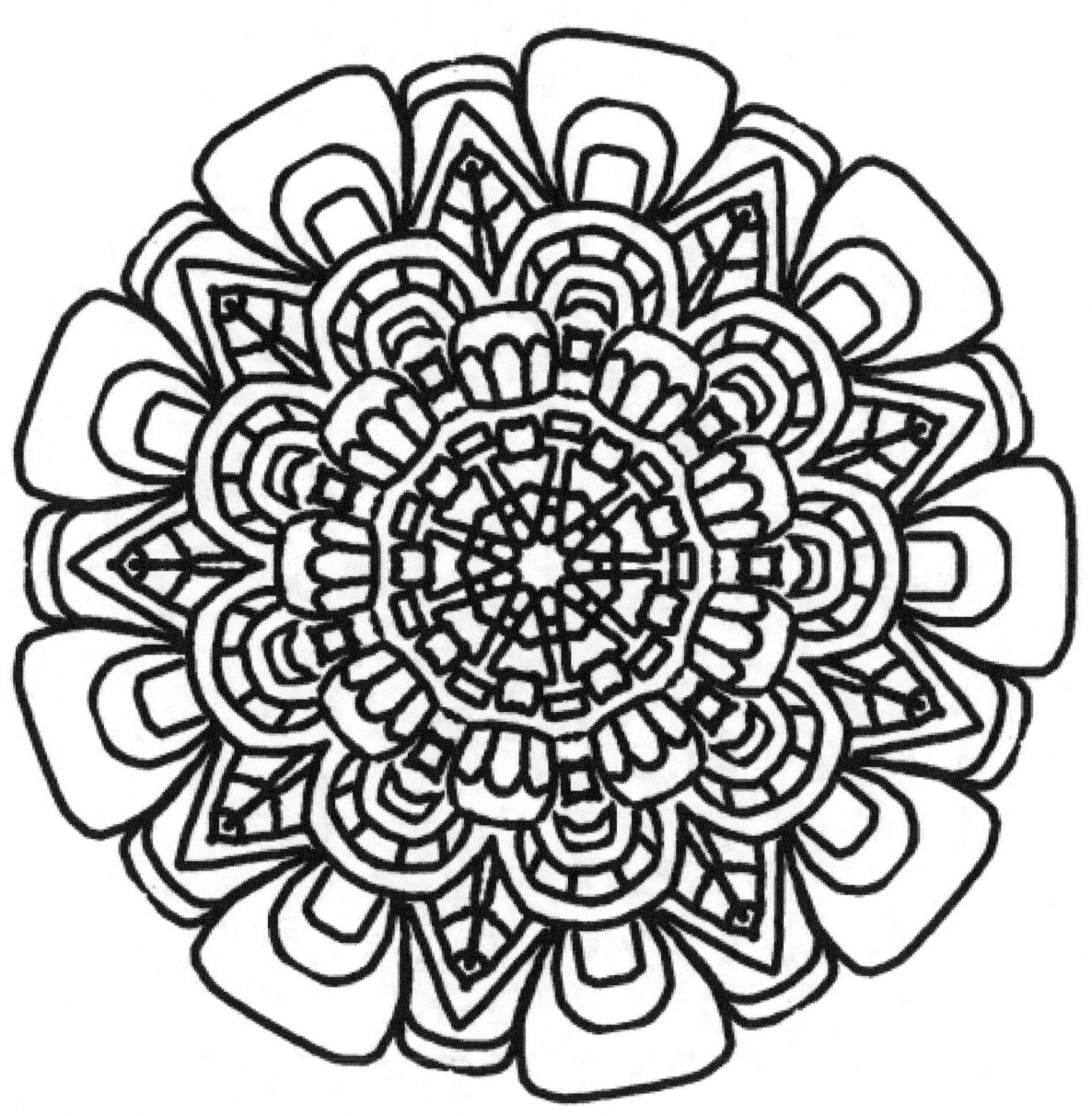

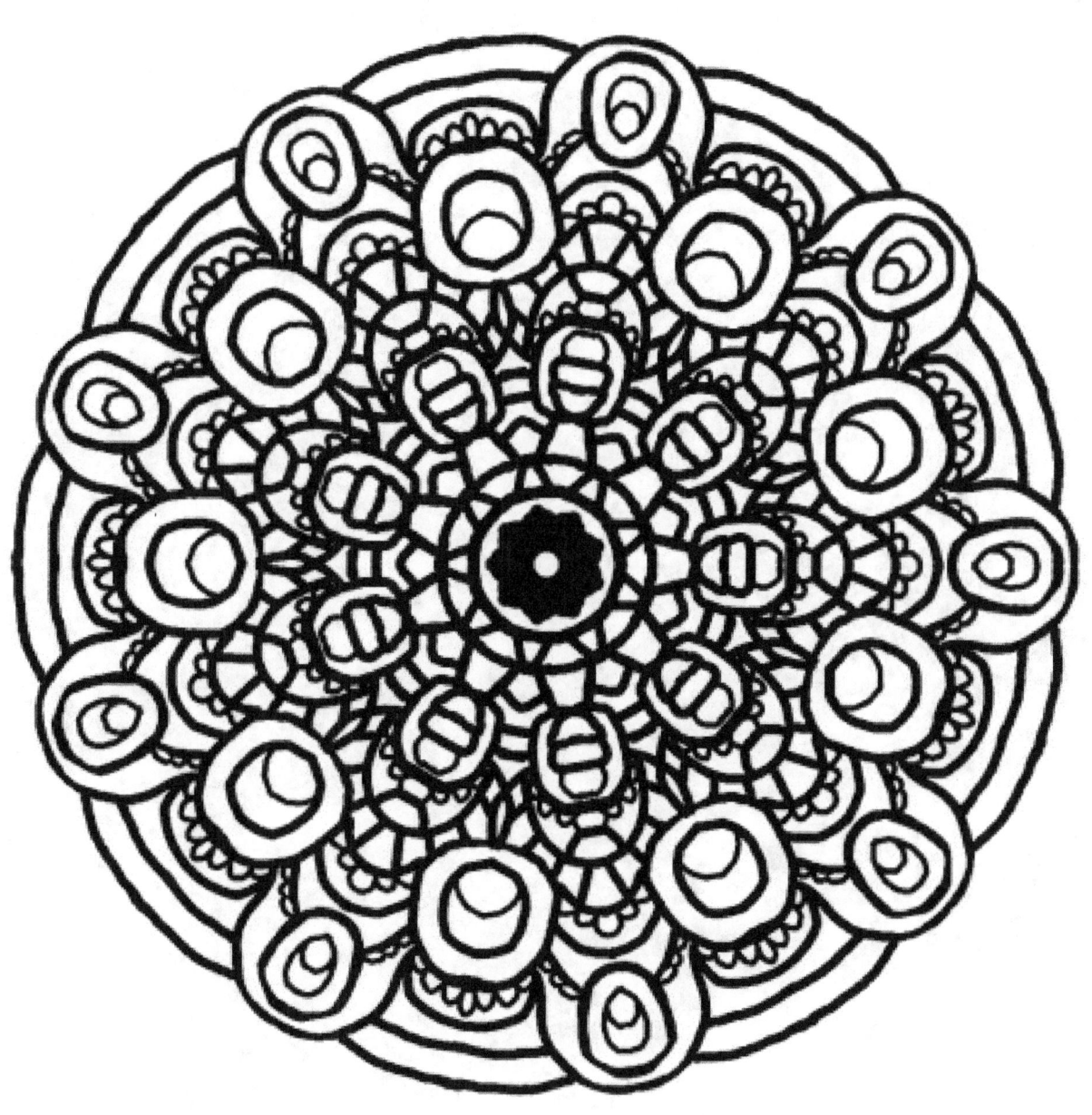

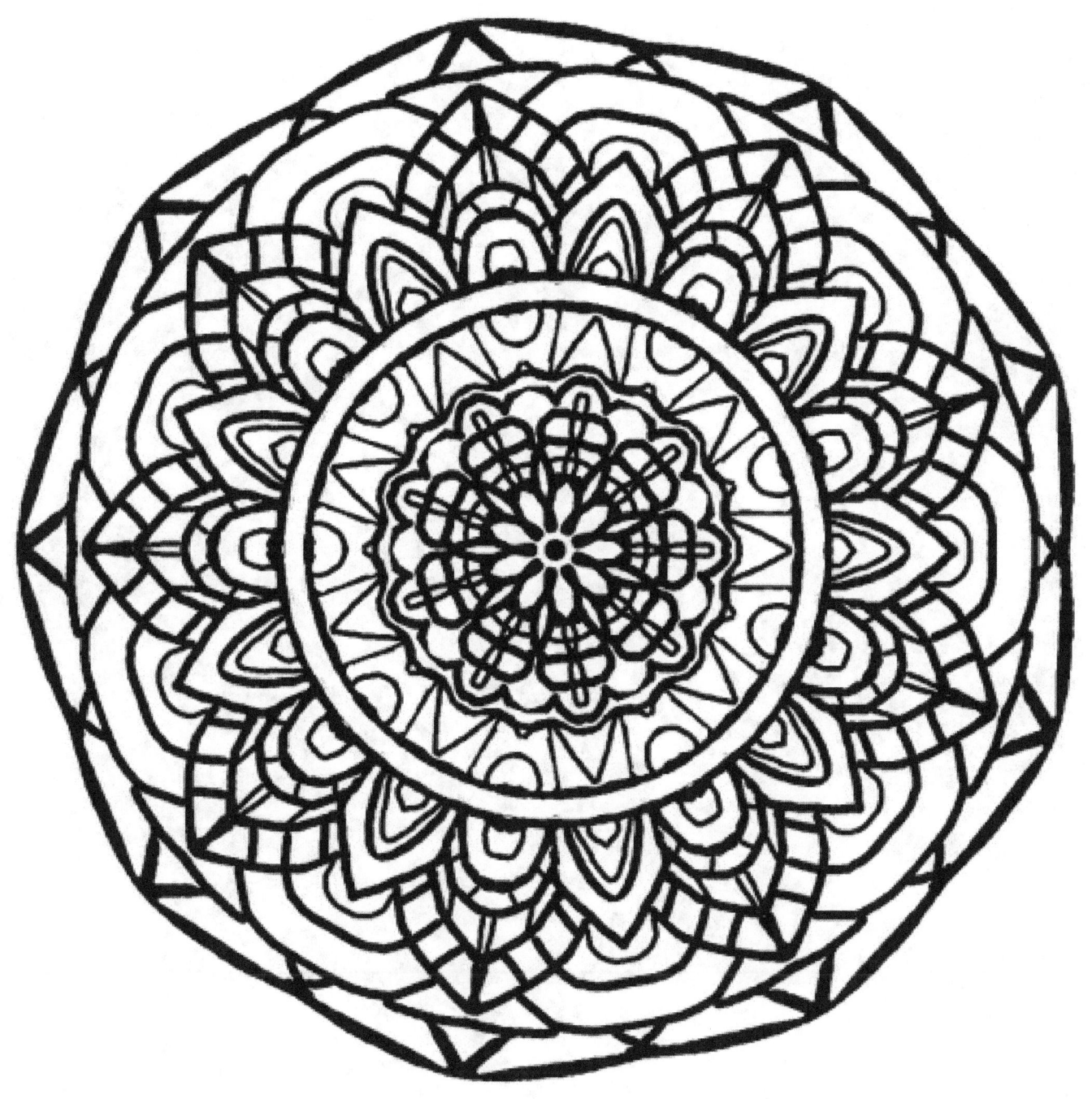

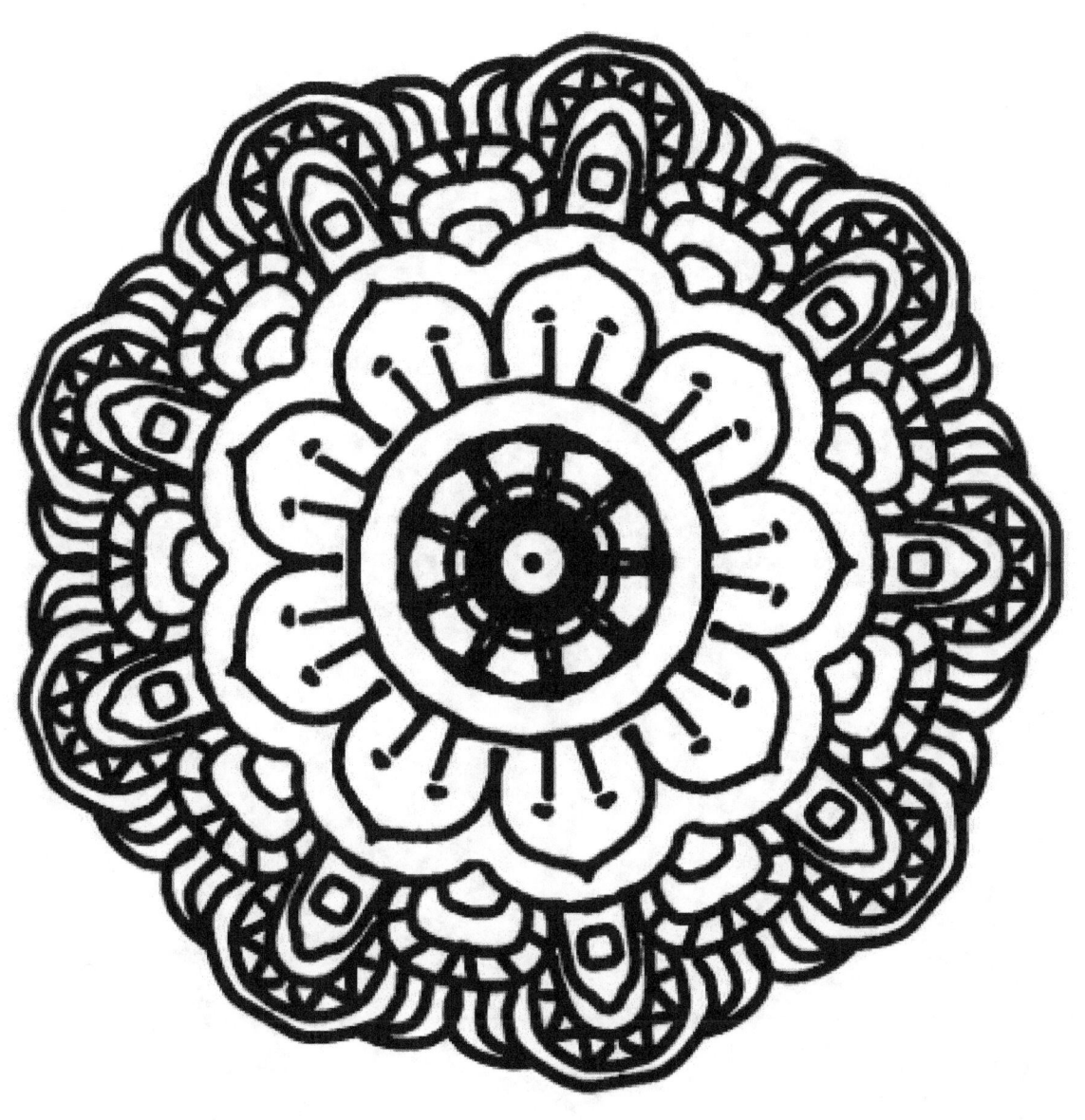

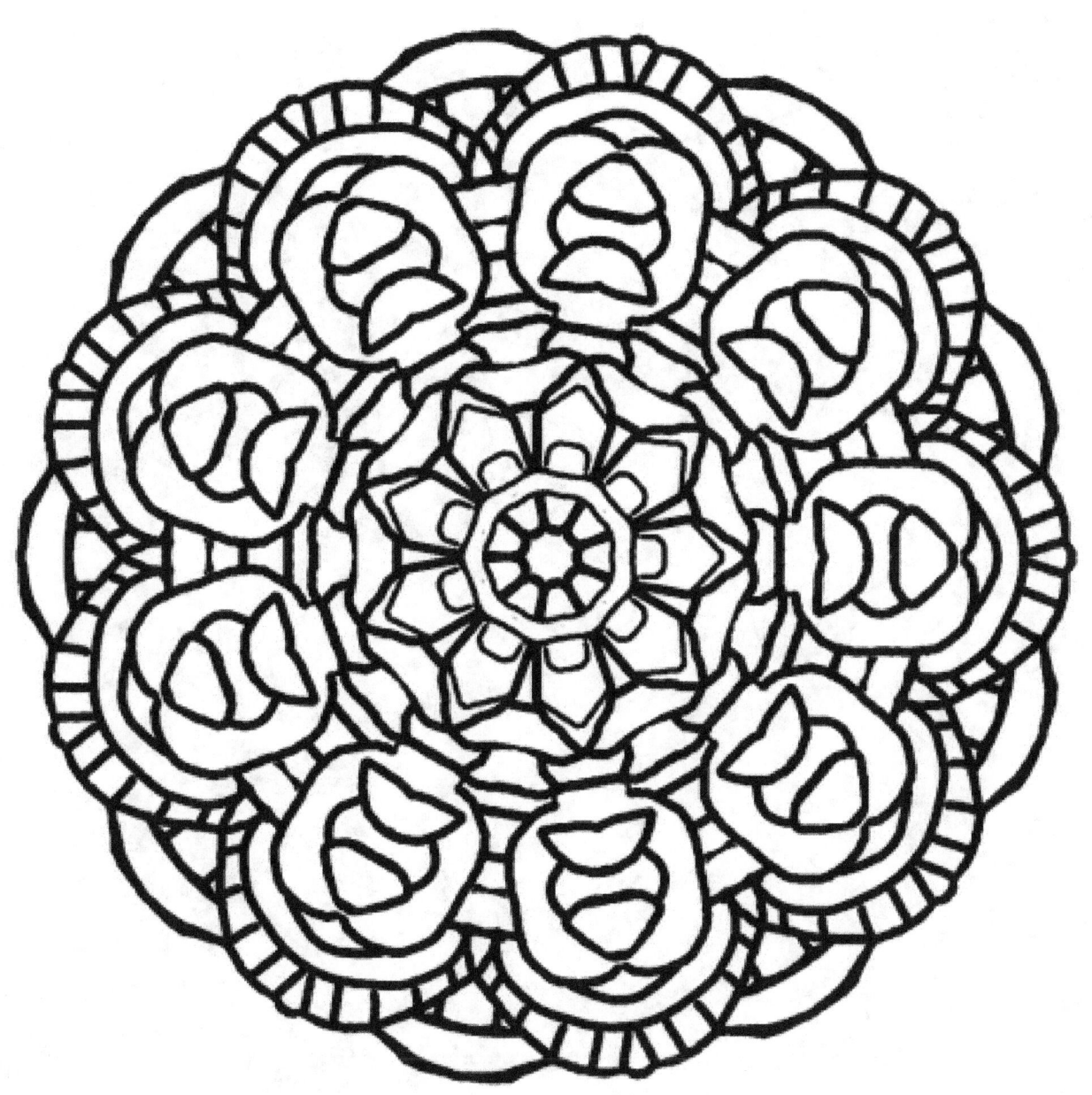

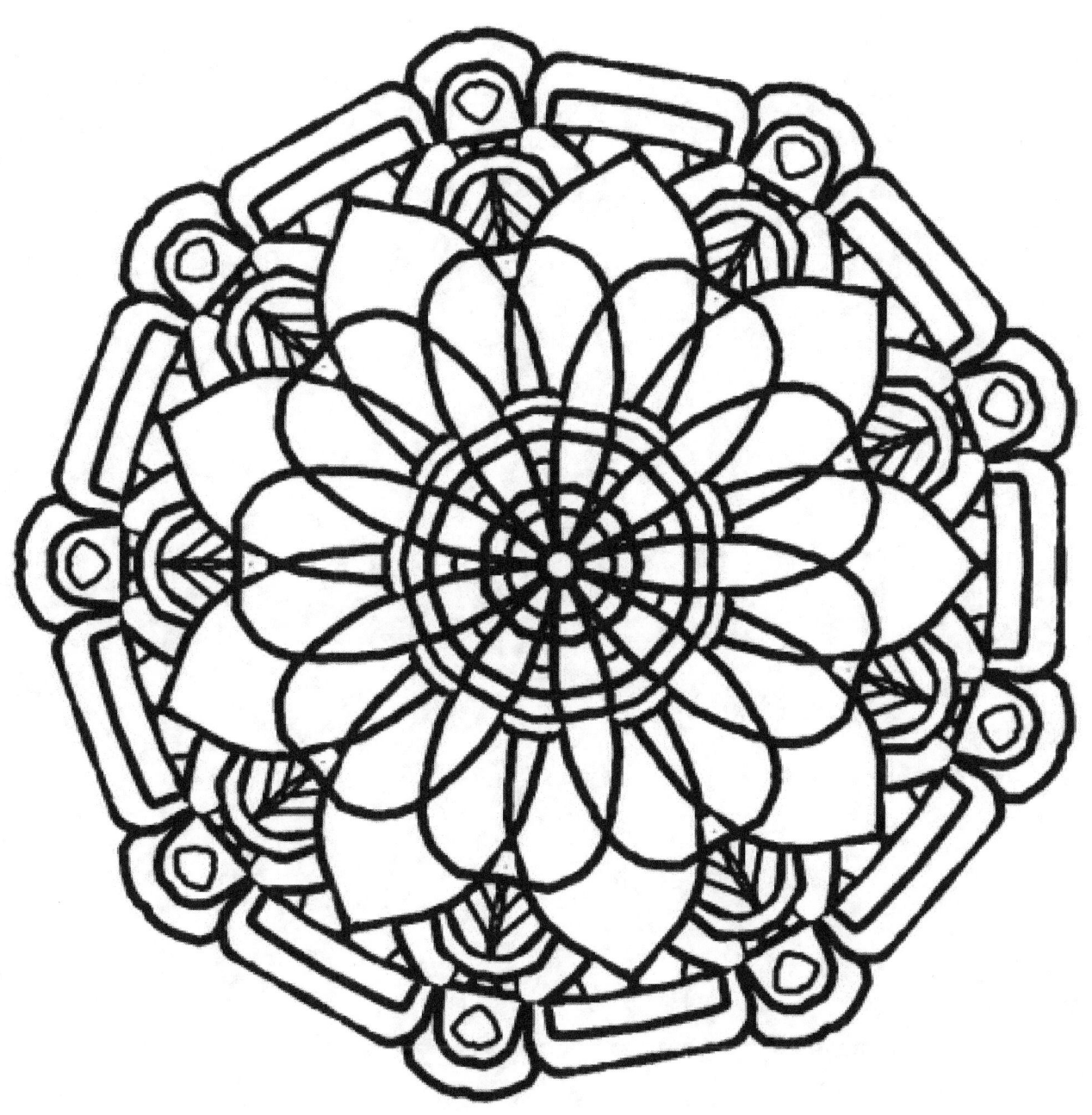

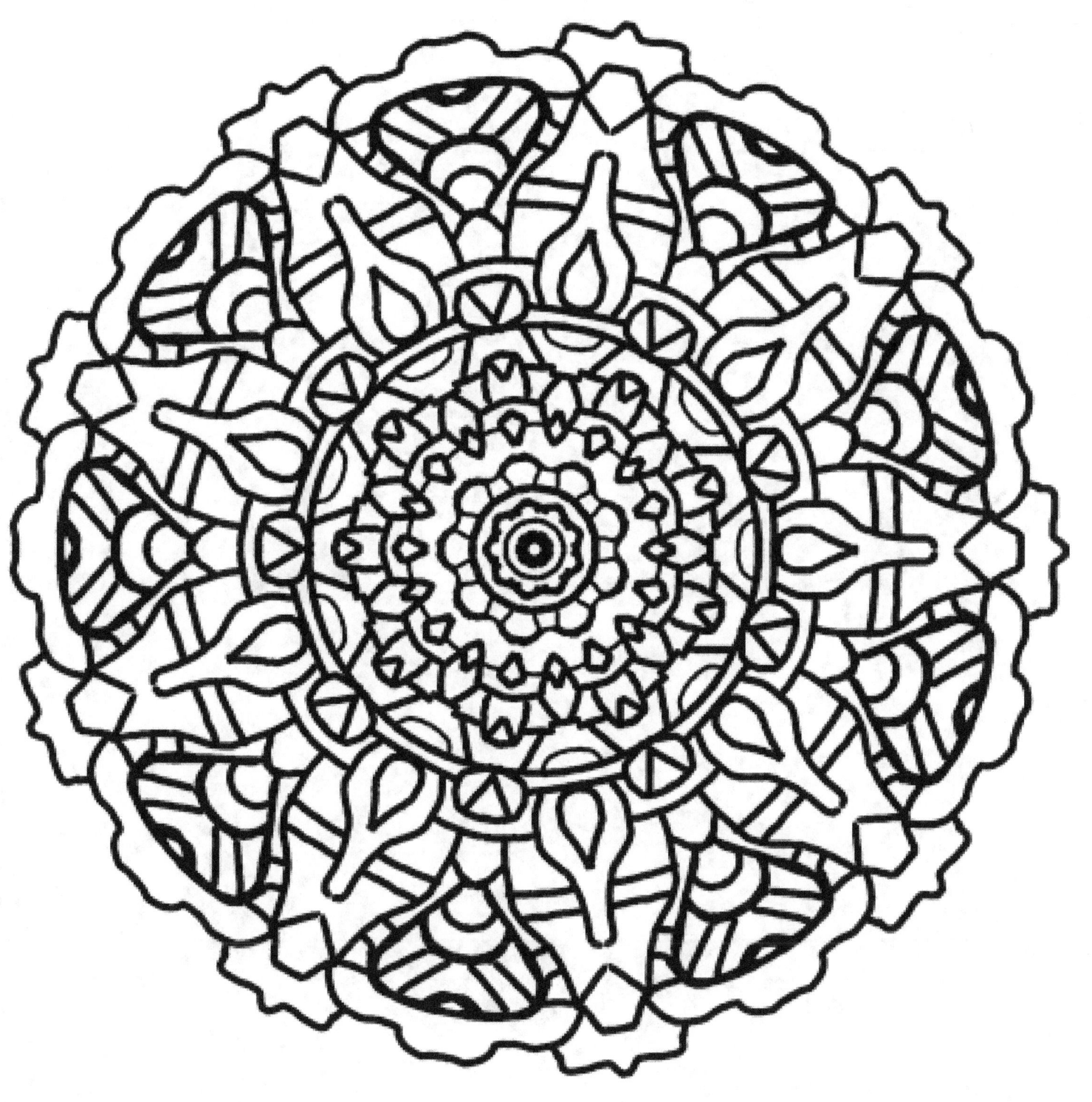

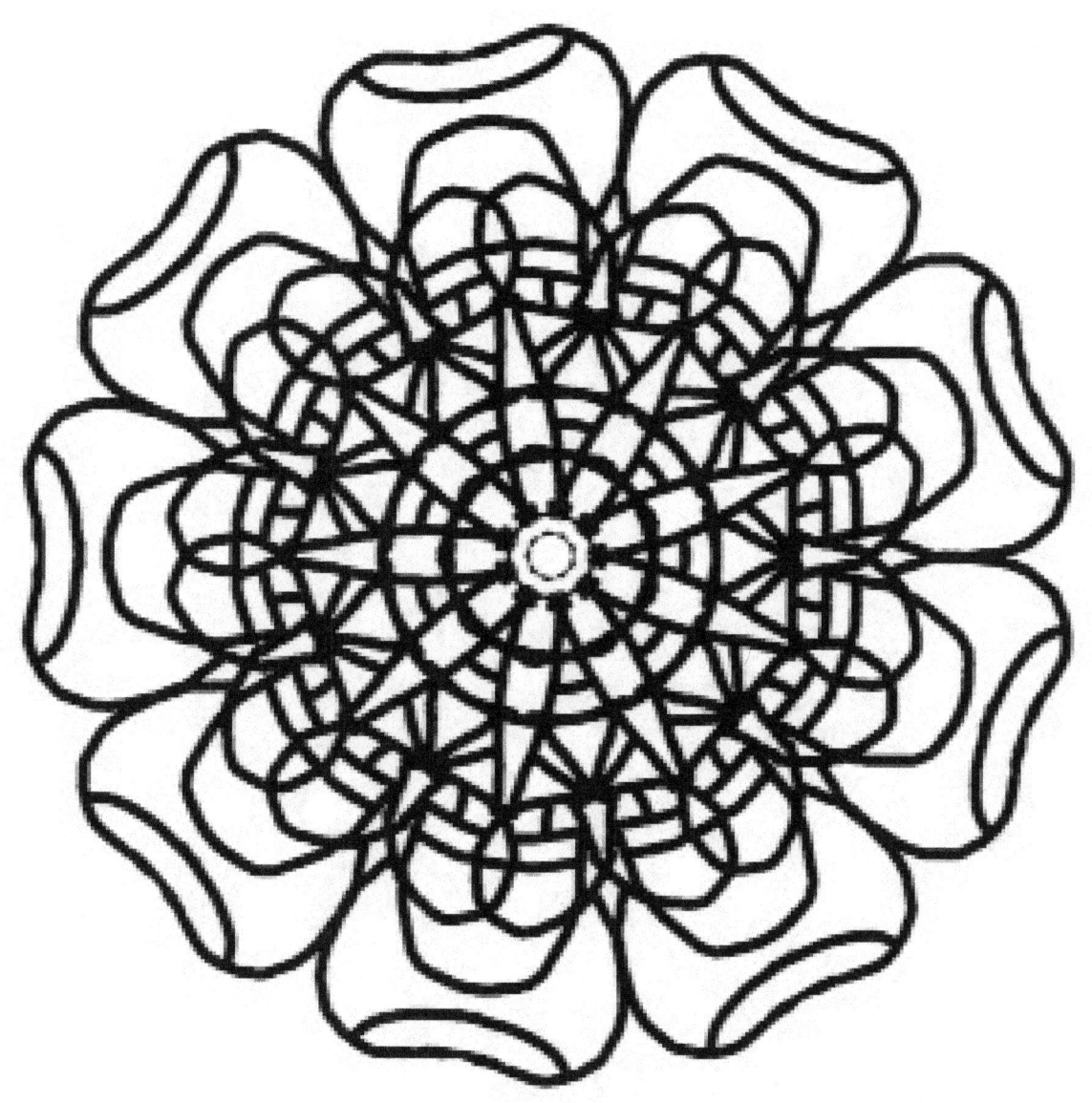

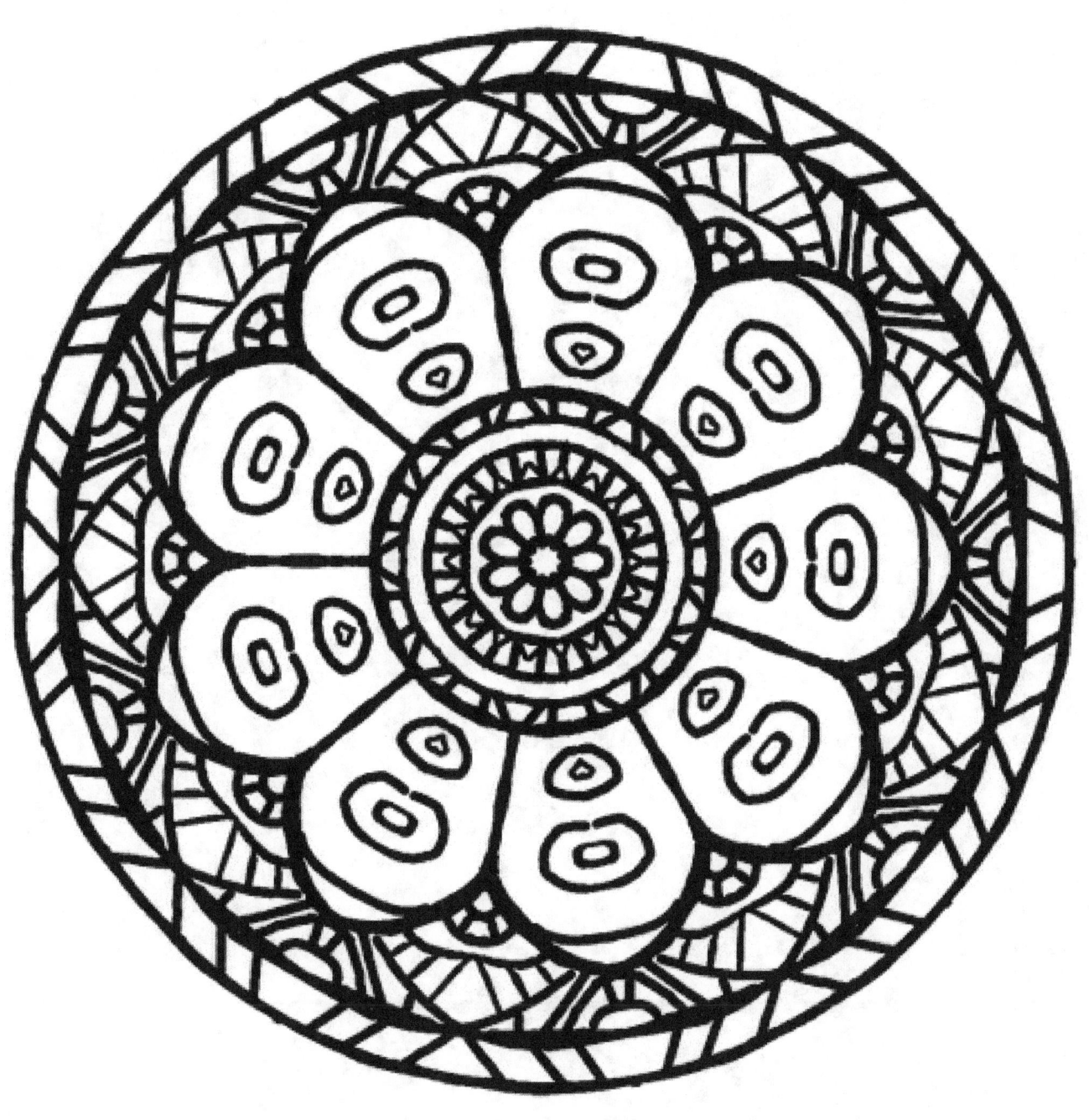

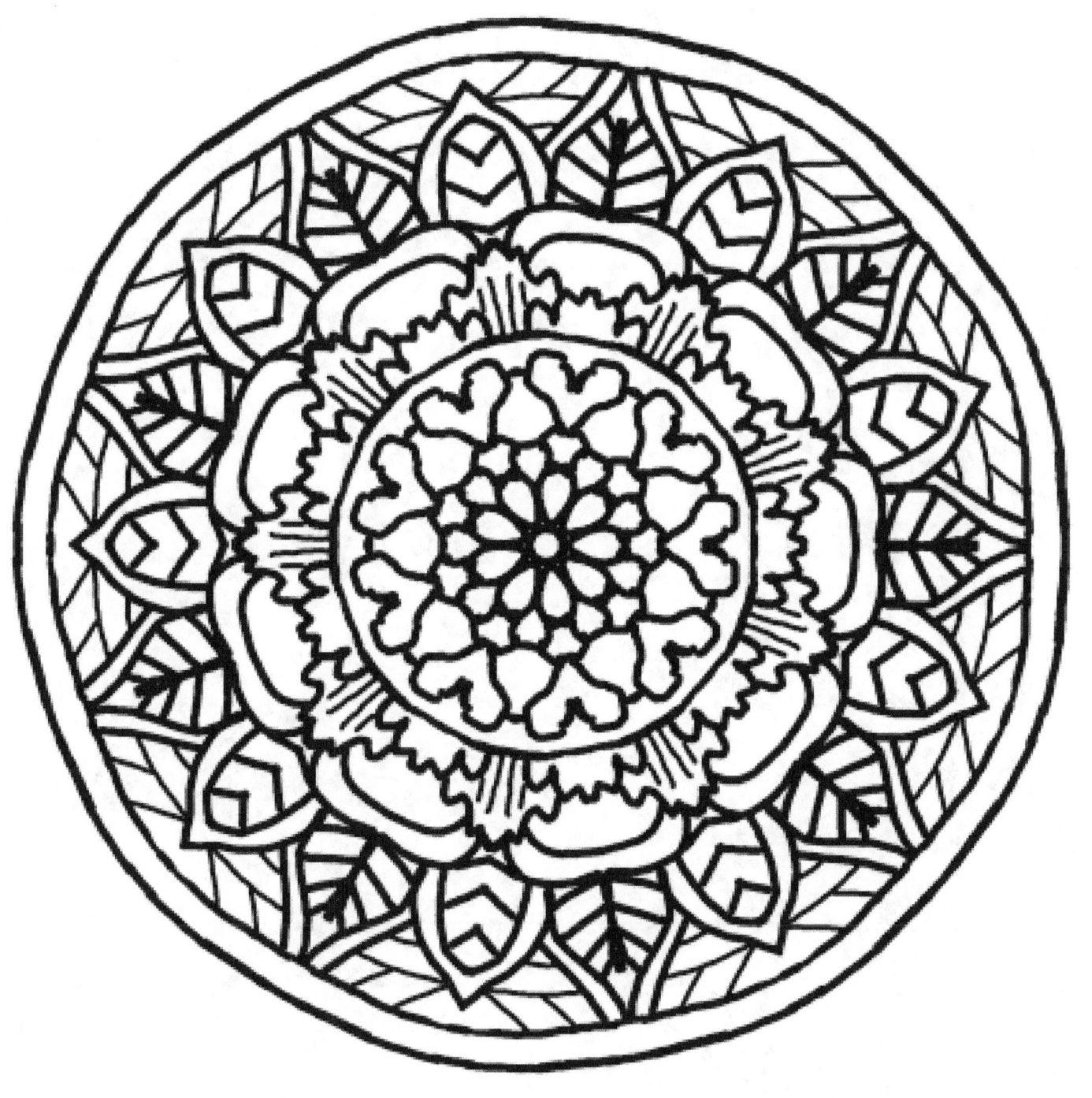

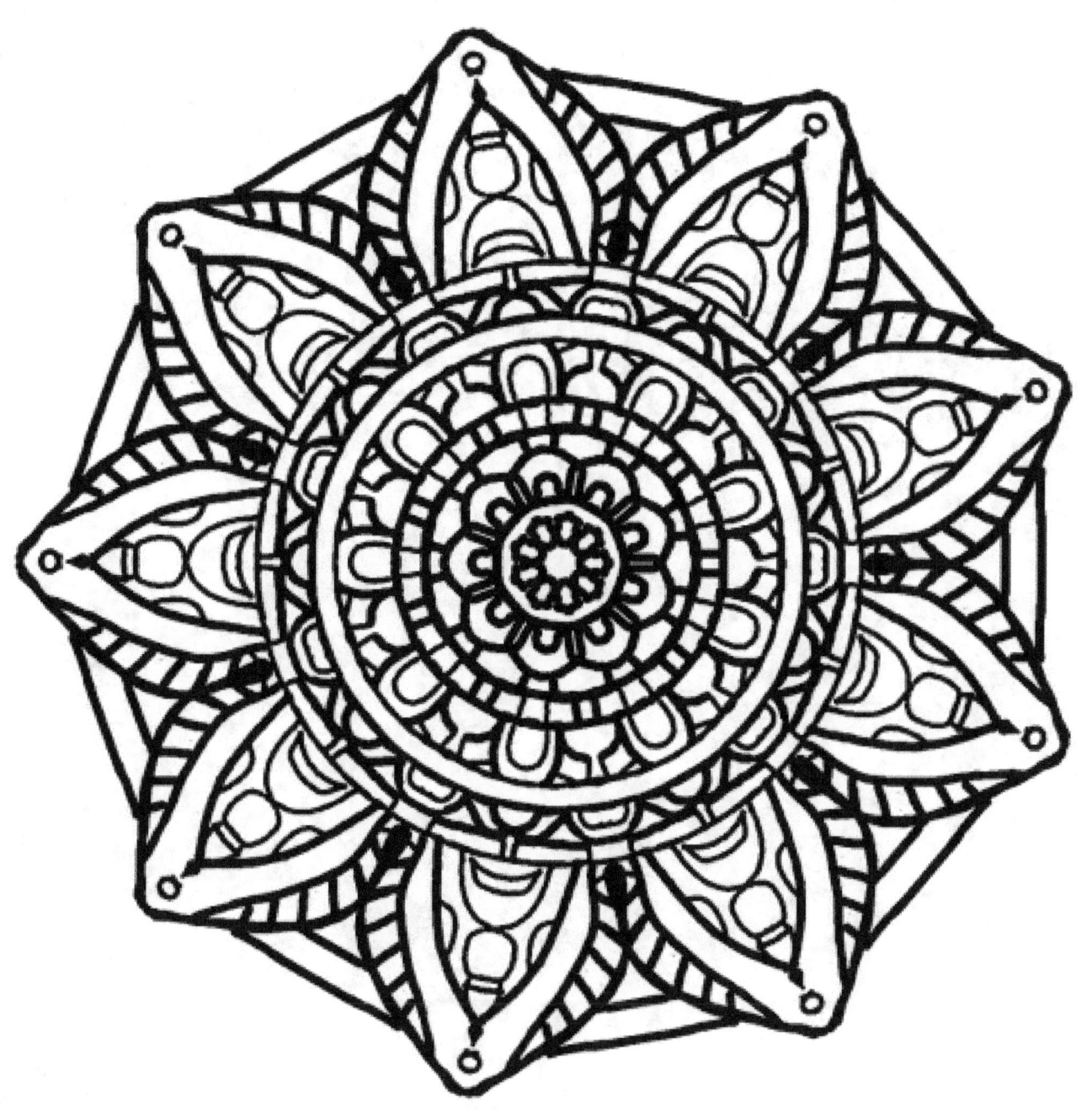

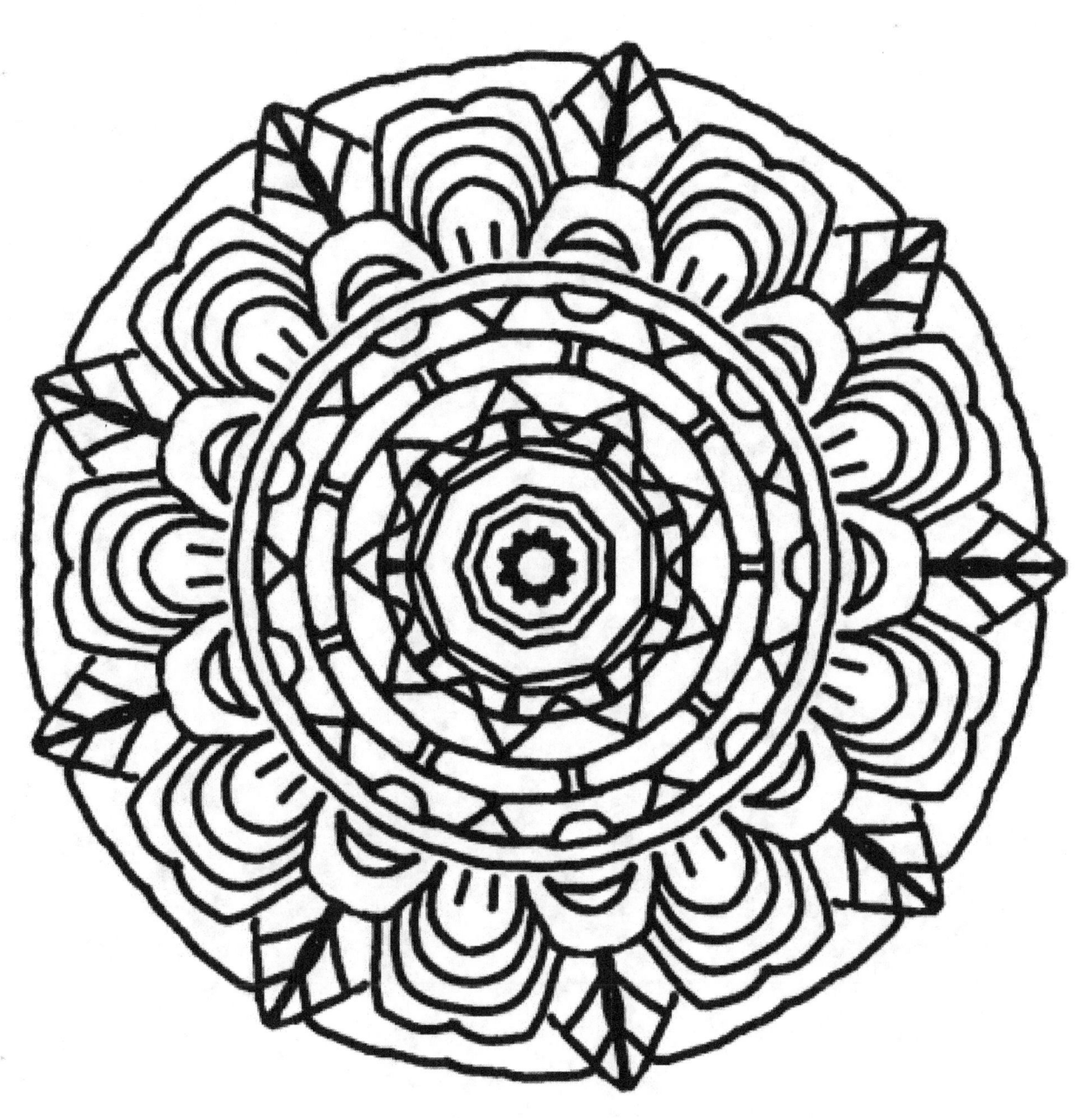

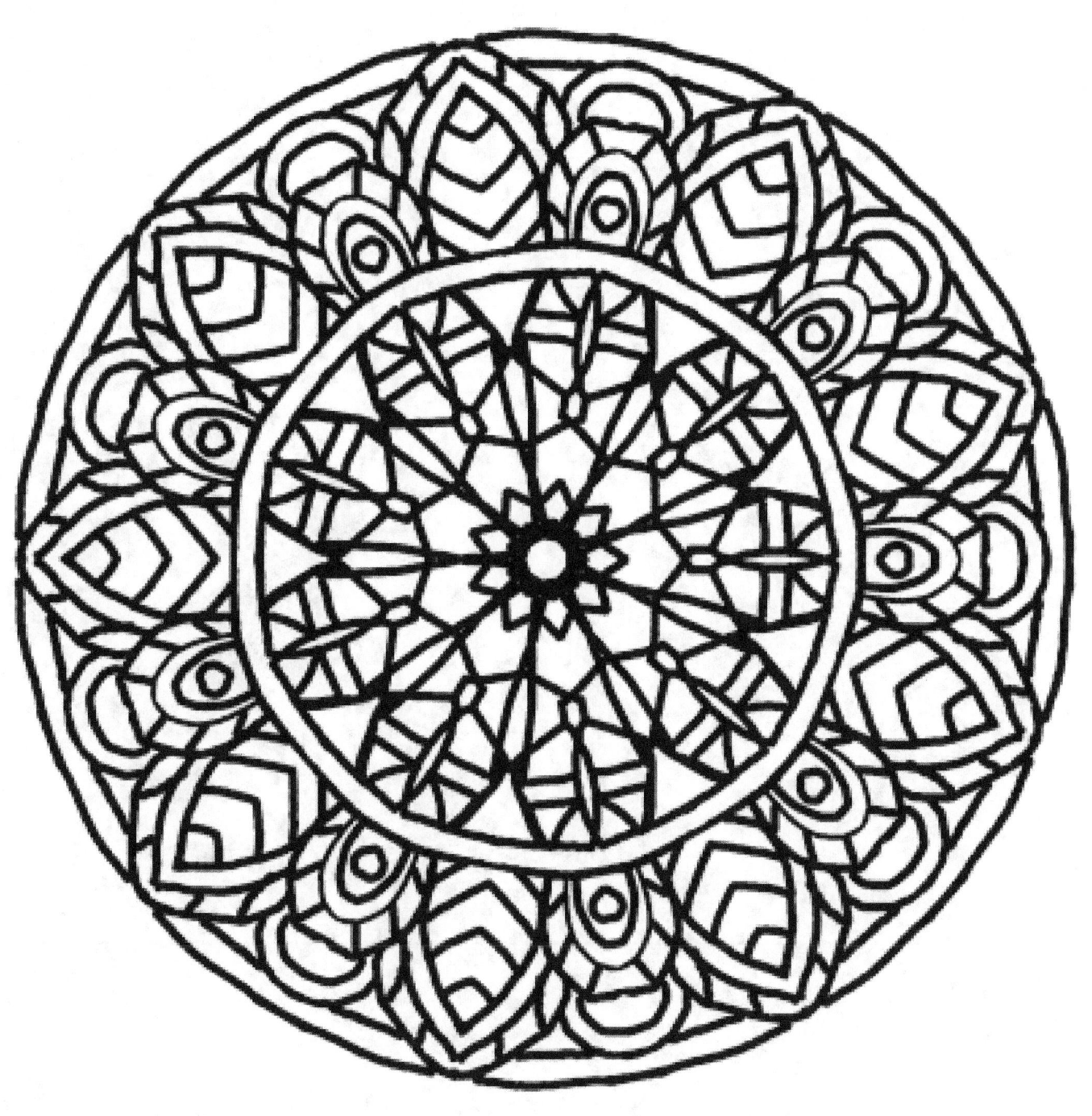

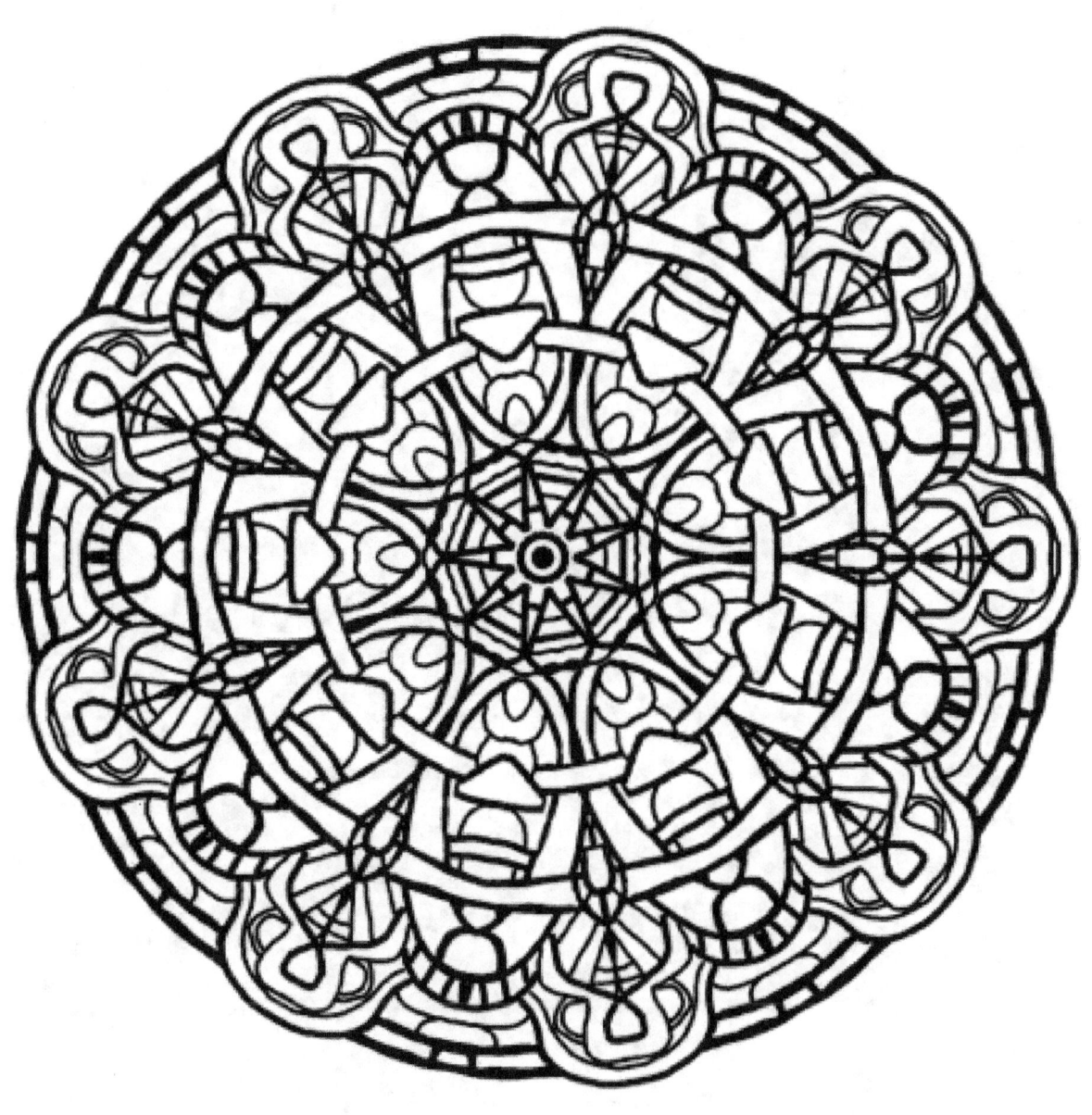

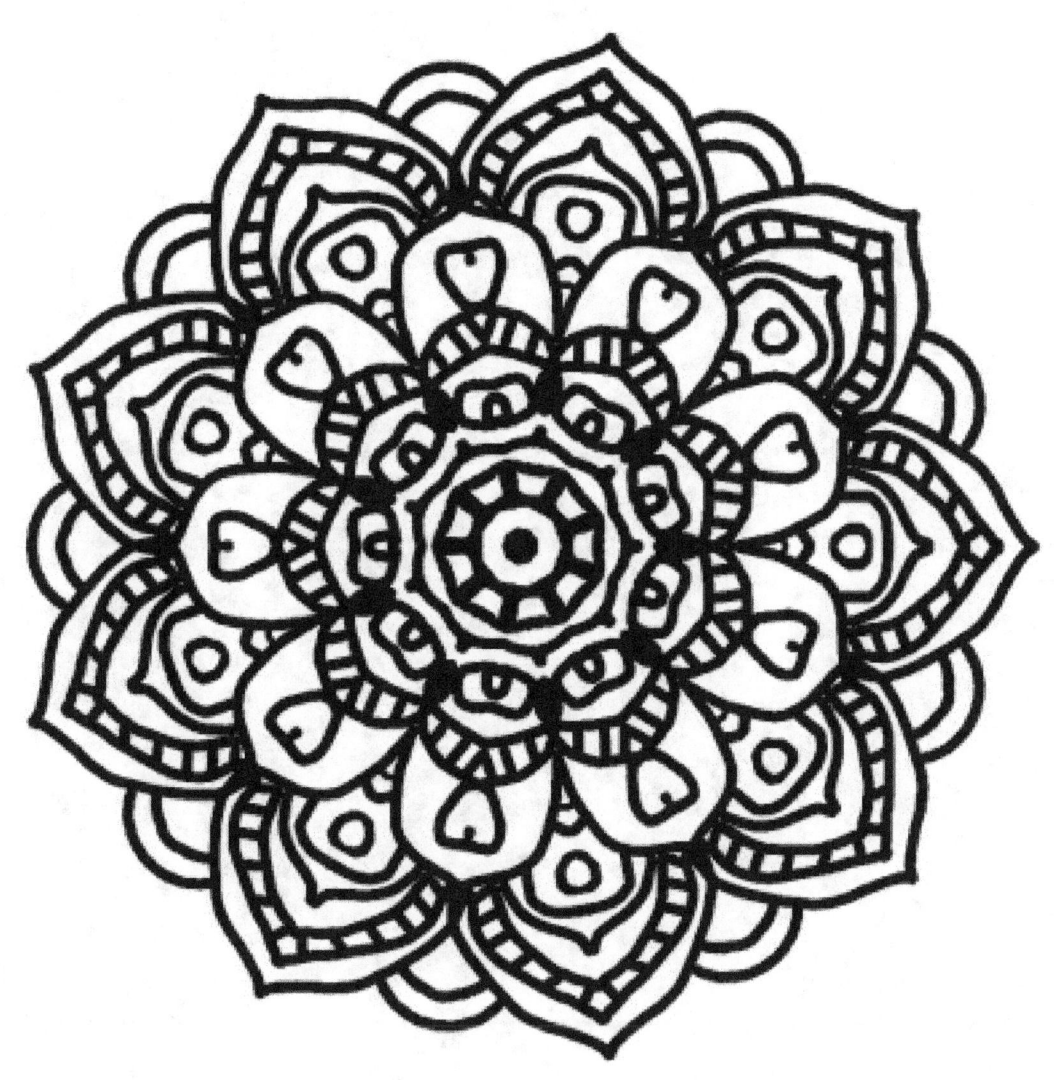

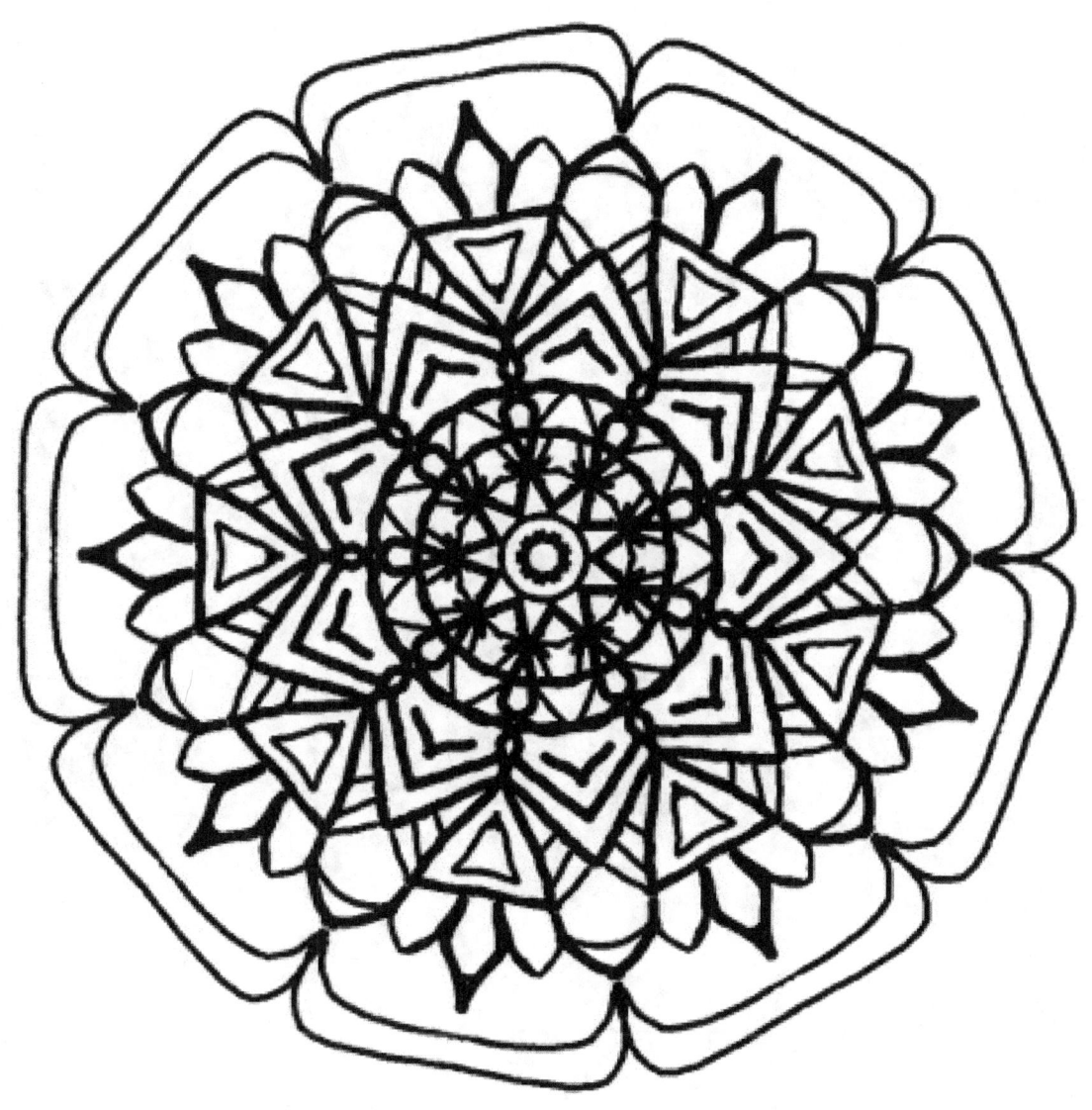

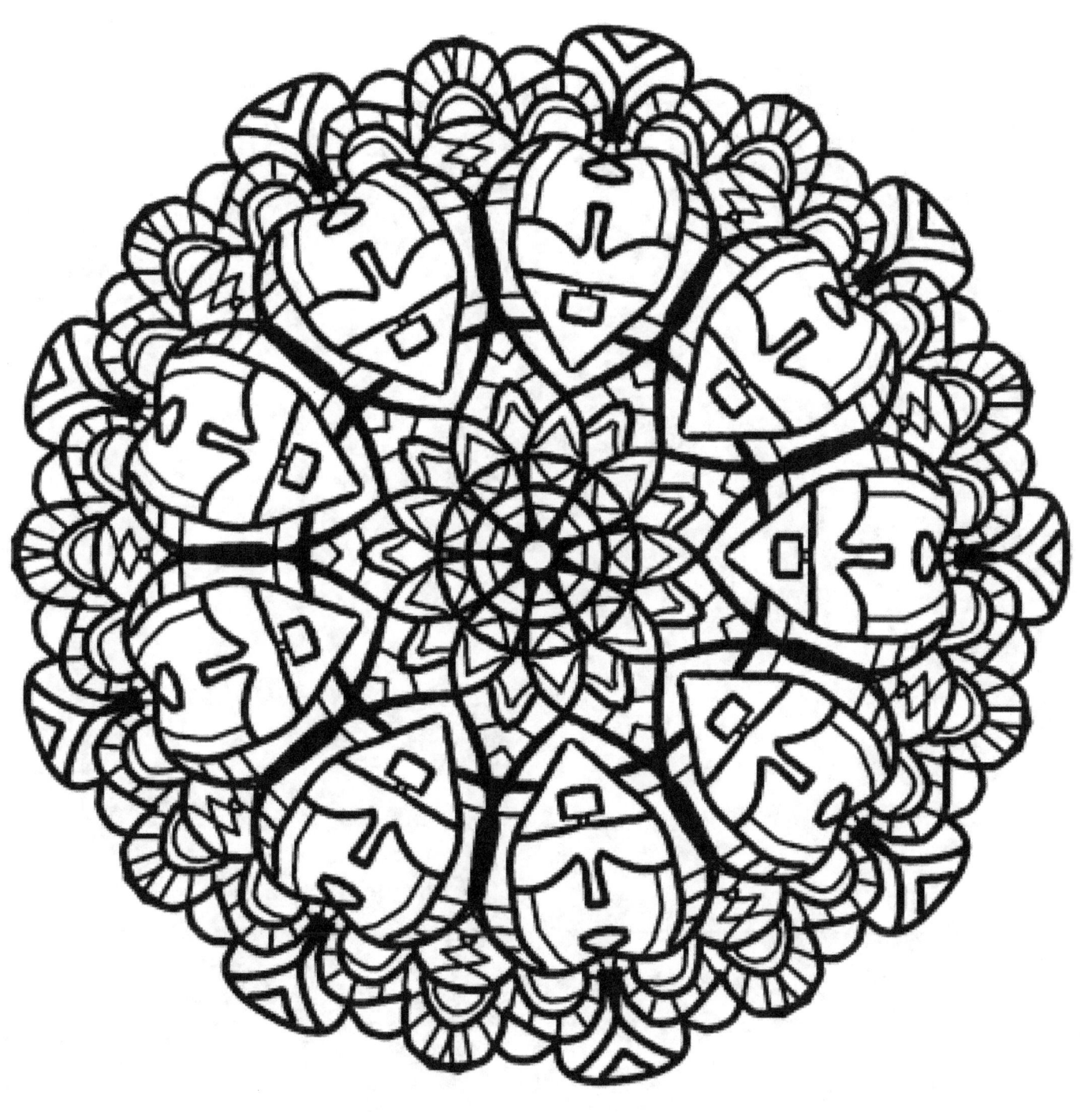

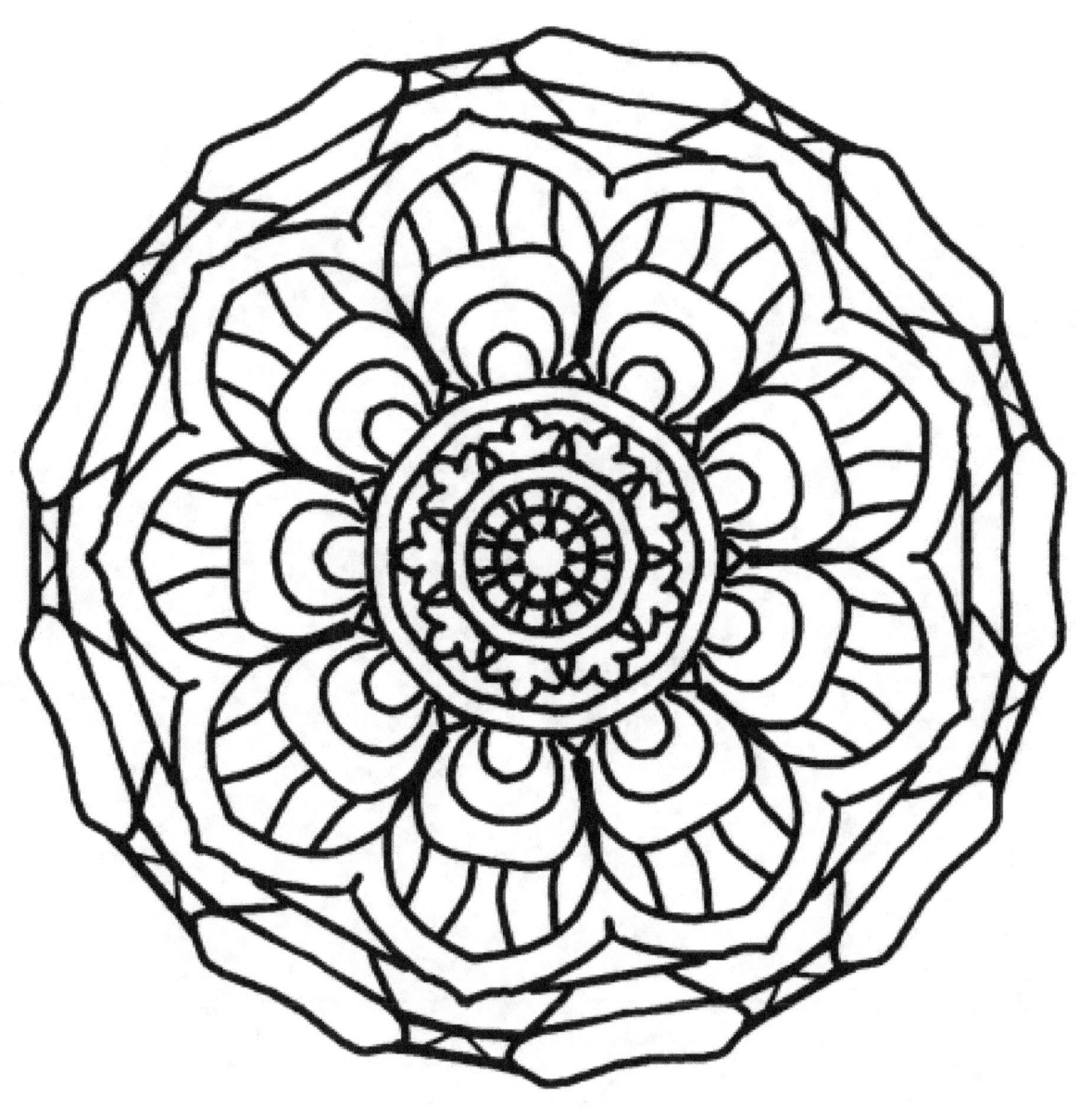

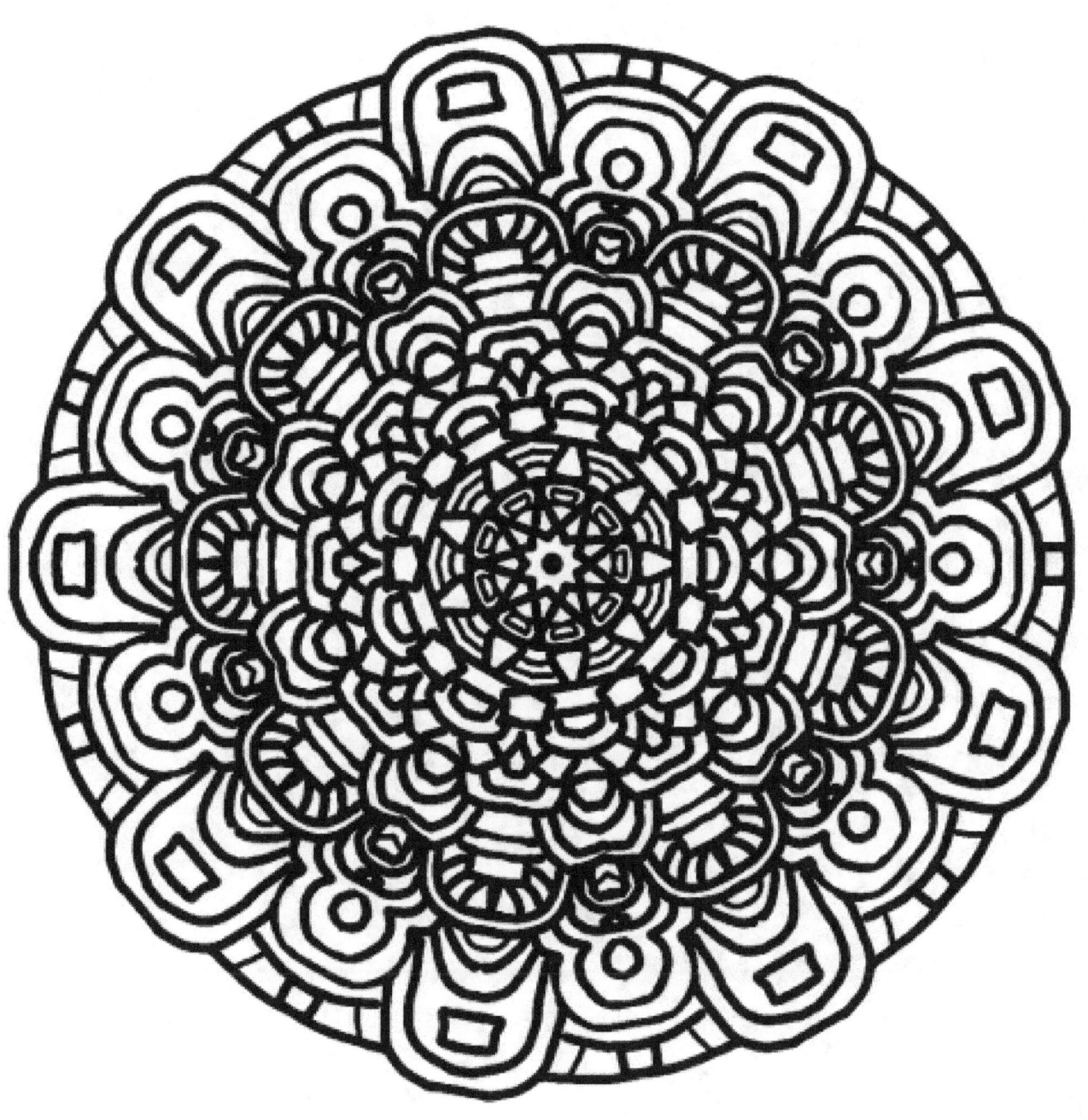

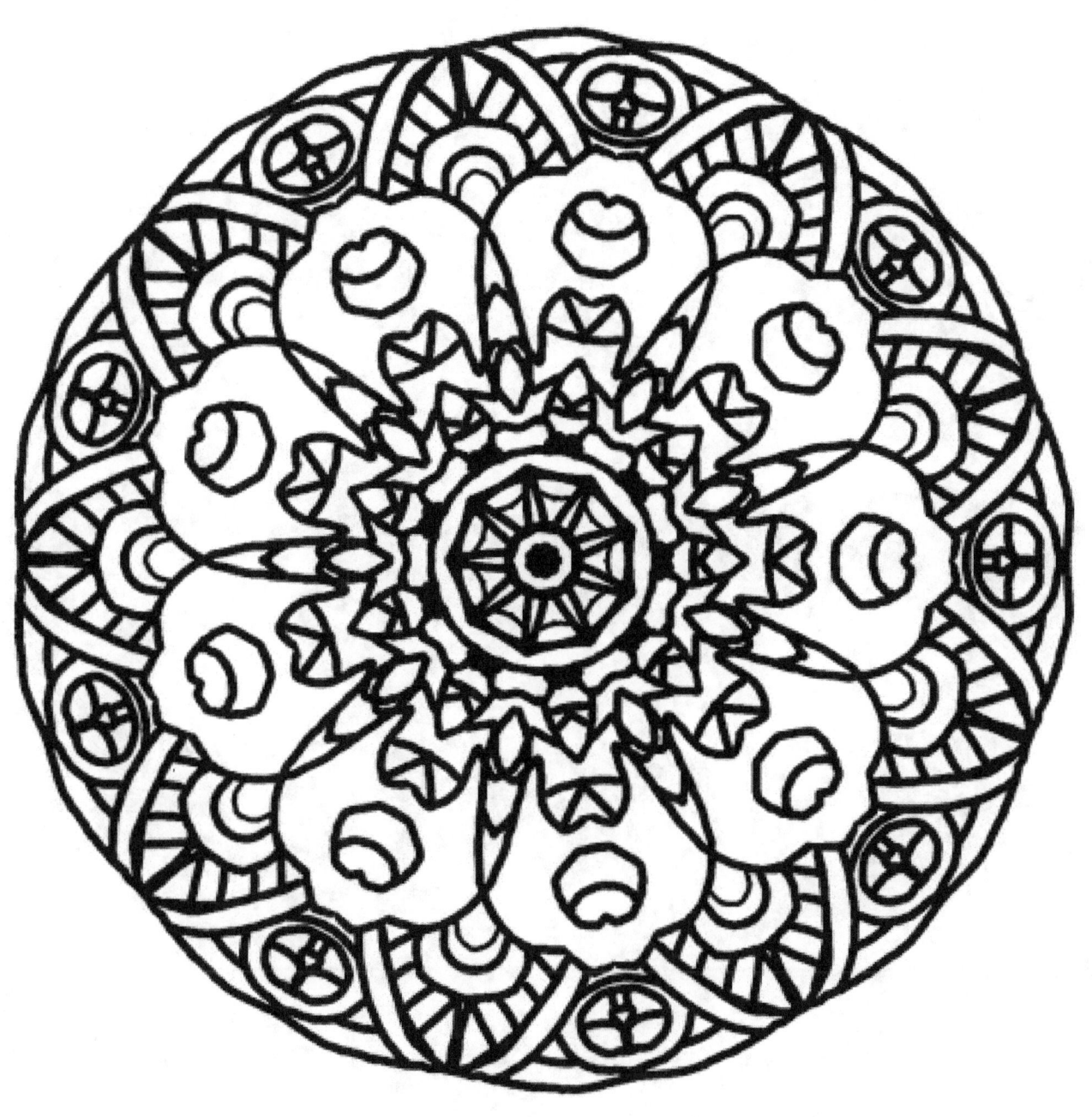

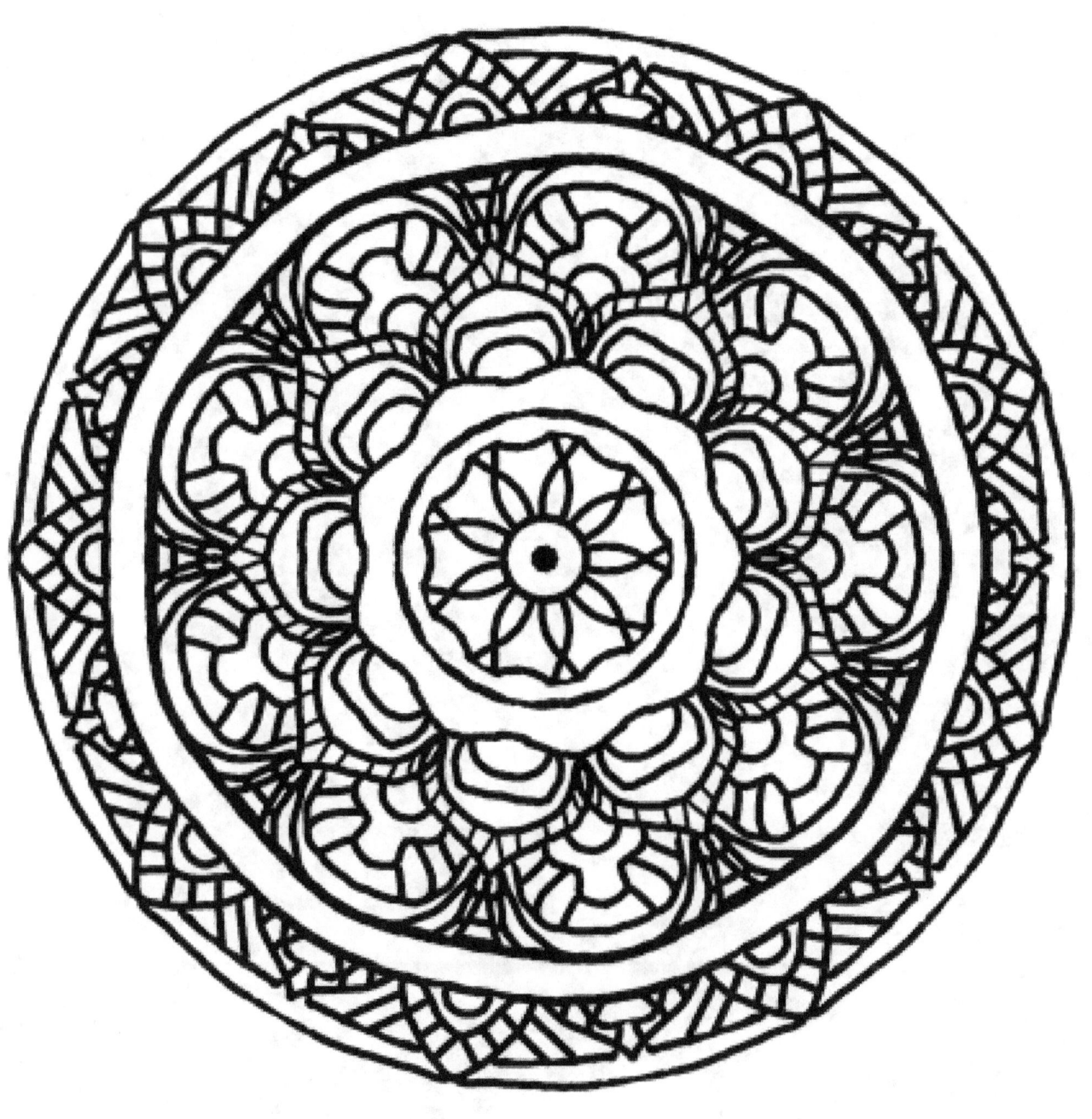

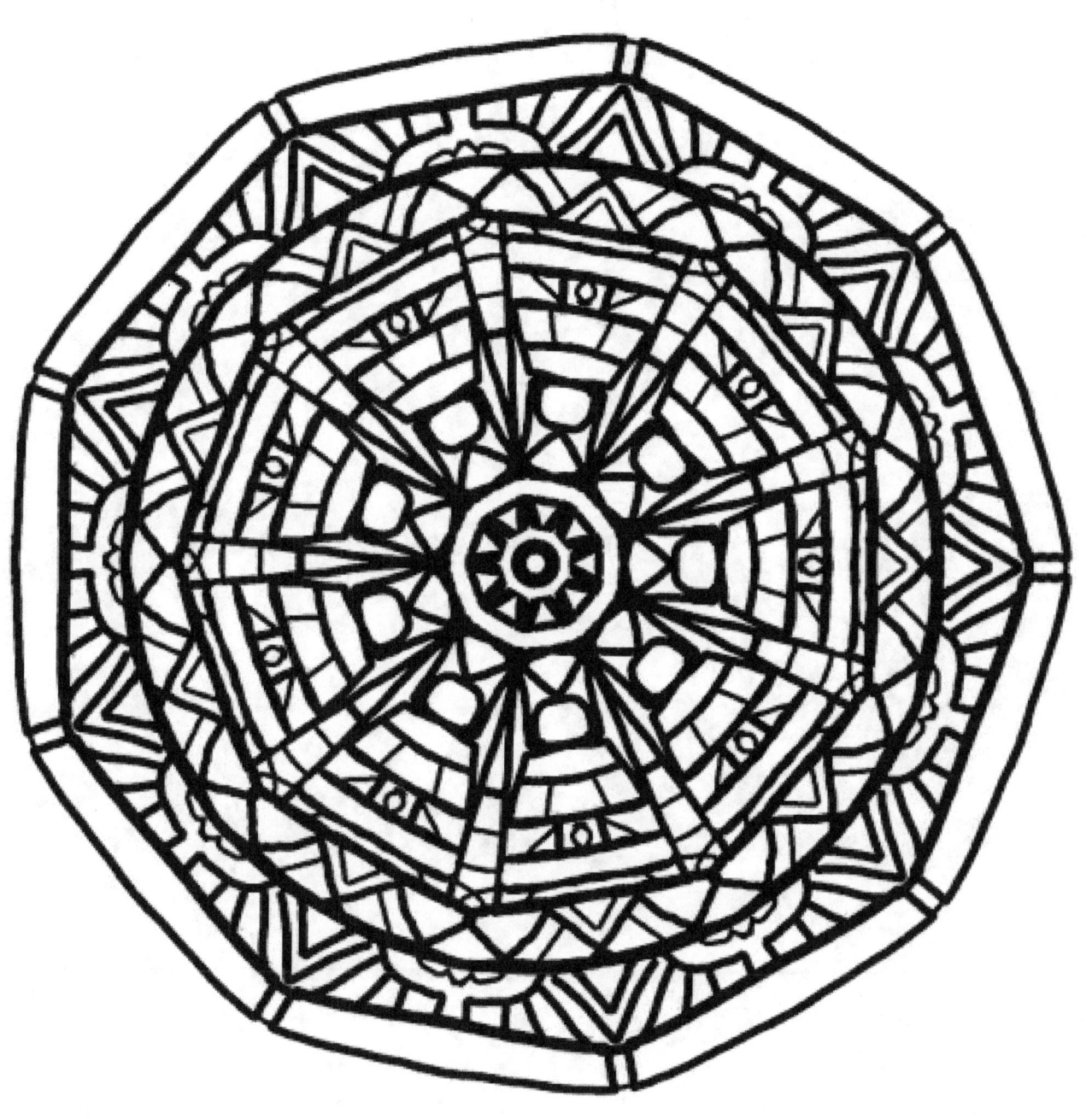

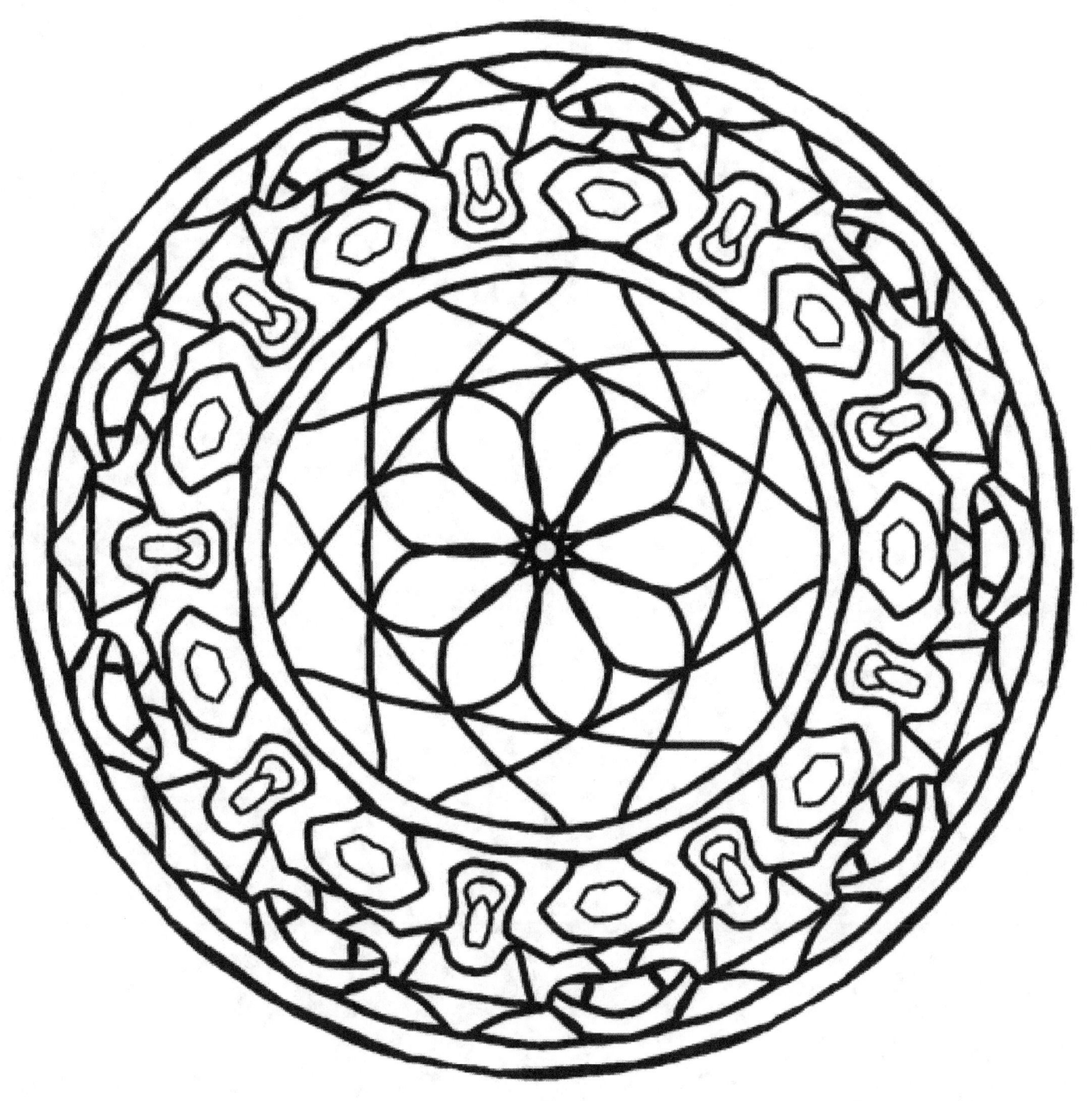

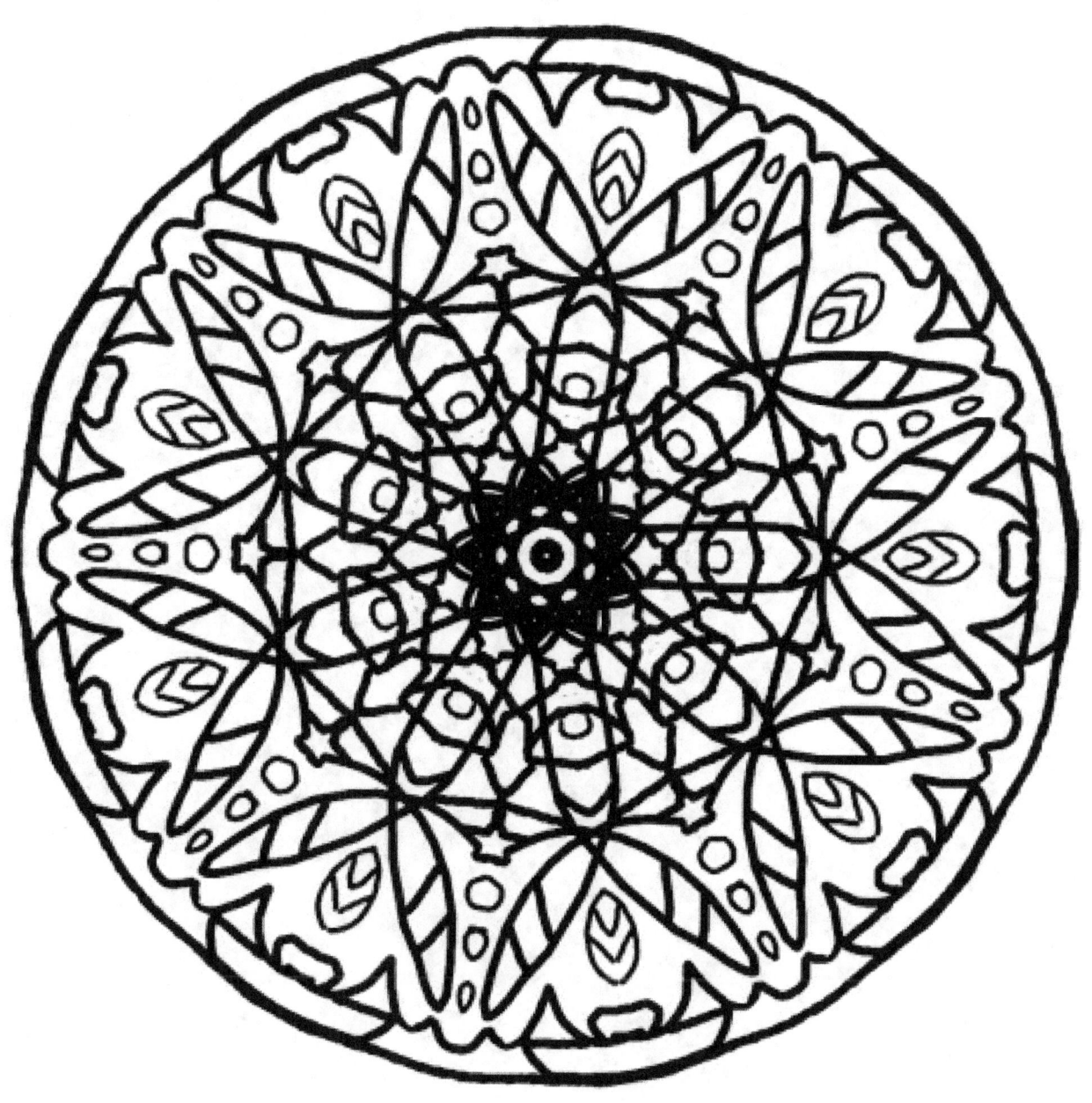

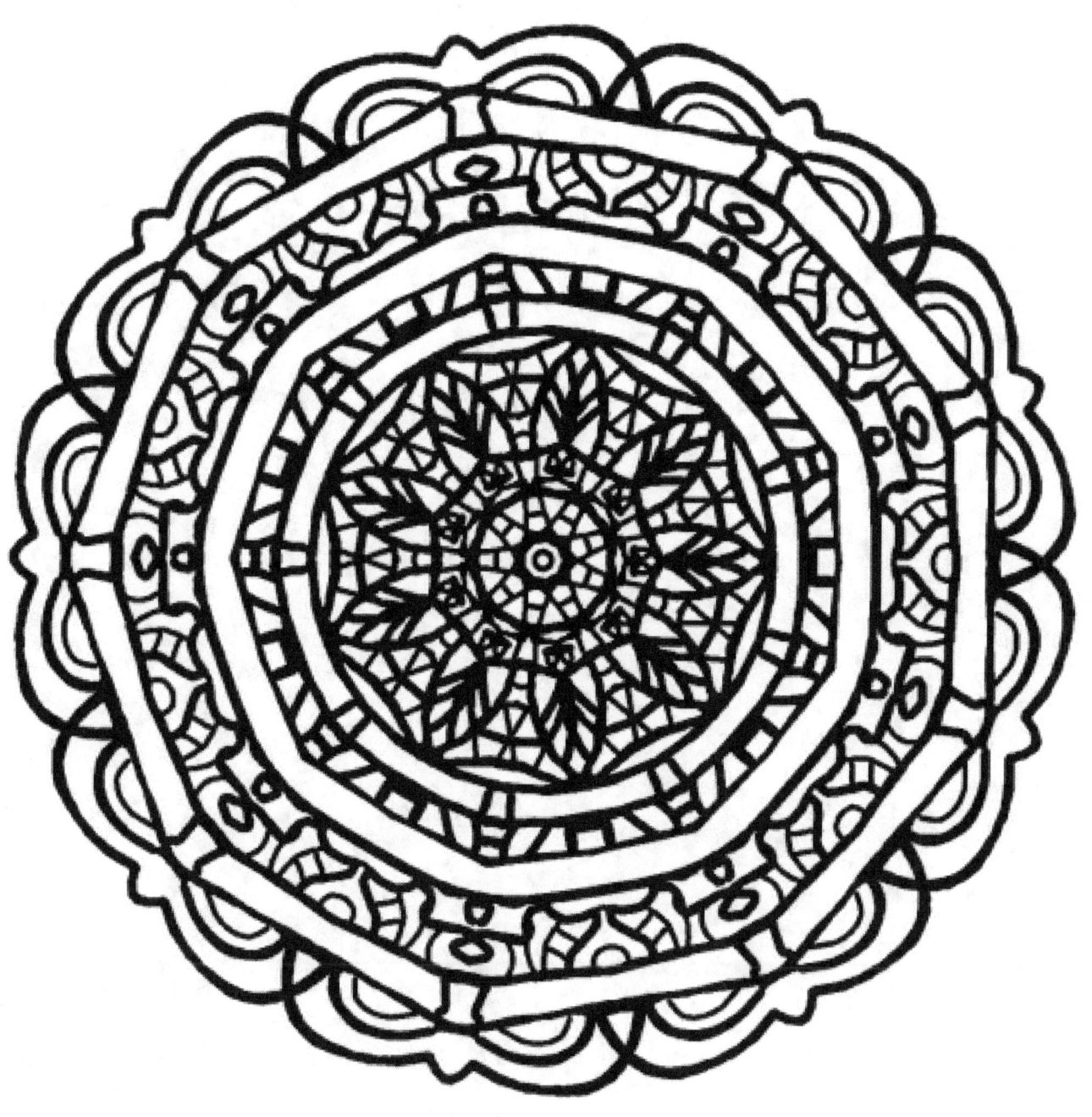

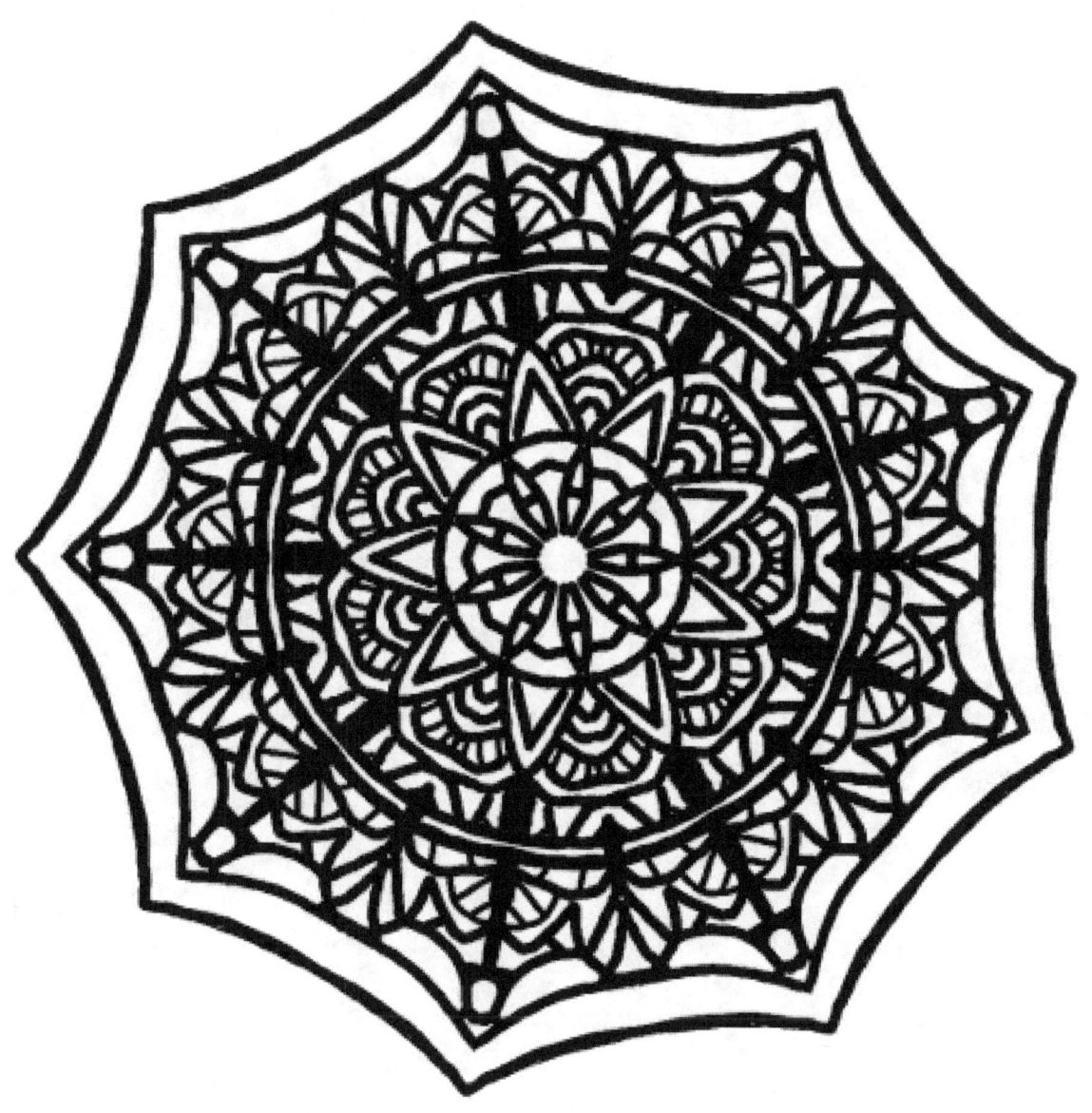

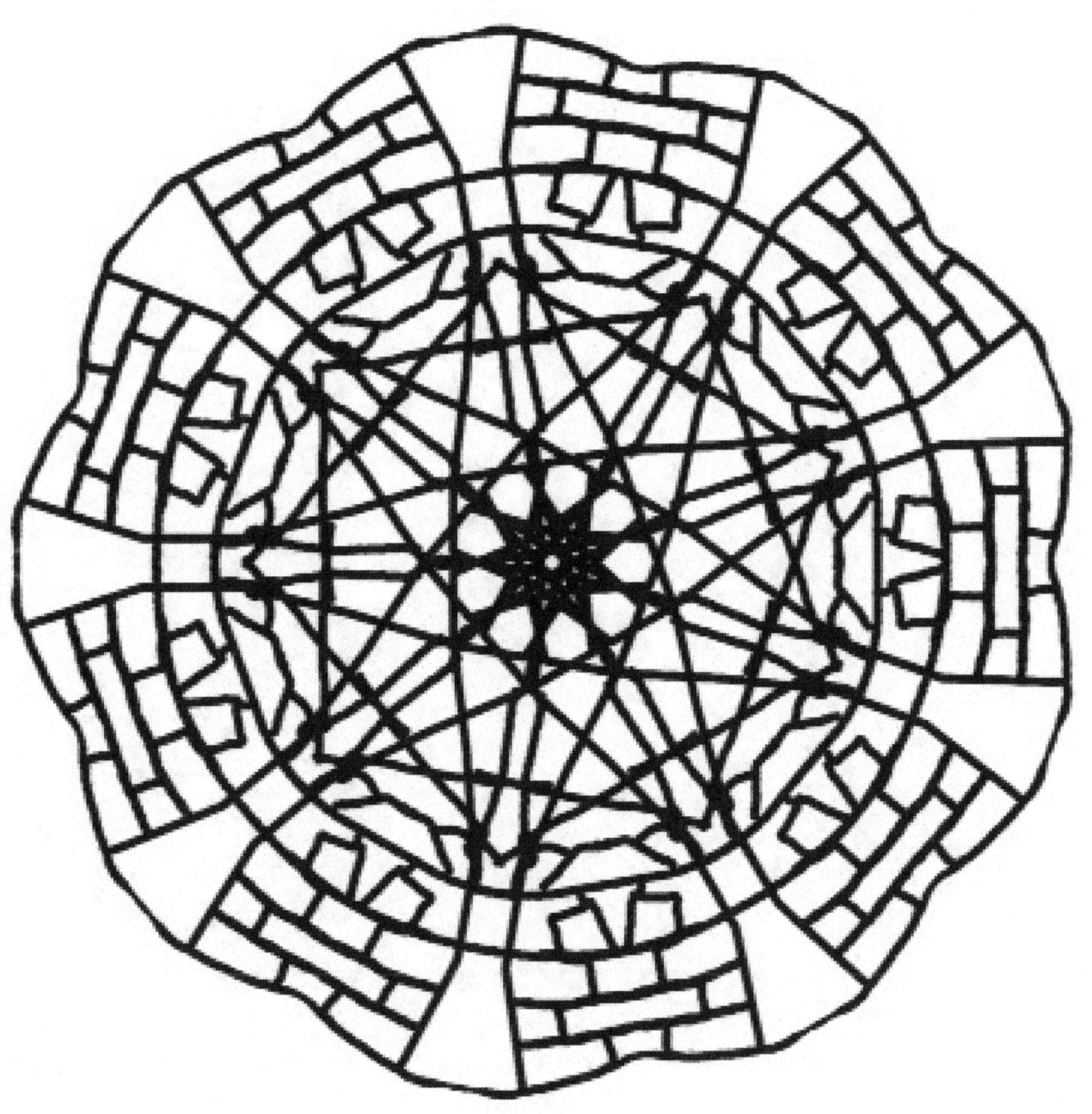

Test Your Colors Here!

Look For Other Relaxing Coloring Books From The Serenity Reiki Clinic

- Relaxation
- Problem Solving
- Restful Sleep
- Healing With Color

Visit WWW.SERENITYREIKICLINIC.COM or Amazon to order your set today!